Make 'Em Happy. Fix it Fast!

BUSY  WOMAN'S
Quick & Easy Recipes

Busy Woman's Quick & Easy Recipes
Make 'Em Happy. Fix it Fast!

1st Printing - March 2007
2nd Printing - March 2008
3rd Printing - September 2008

International Standard Book No. 978-1-59769-002-7

Library of Congress No. 2007924830

Illustrations by Nancy Bohanan

Edited, Designed and Published in the United States of America
and Manufactured in China by
Cookbook Resources, LLC
541 Doubletree Drive
Highland Village, Texas 75077
Toll free 866-229-2665

www.cookbookresources.com

cookbook
resources LLC
Bringing Family and Friends to the Table

BUSY WOMAN'S
Quick & Easy Recipes

Busy woman...kind of redundant isn't it?

What woman isn't busy? Look around, can you find one? We couldn't either. Therefore, Cookbook Resources, LLC proudly offers you *Busy Woman's Quick and Easy Recipes,* a collection of time-saving meal ideas that will actually give busy women the opportunity to scratch one thing off of that to-do list each day.

These recipes were tested for taste and ease of preparation right in our own kitchens. From appetizers to entrees or soups to desserts, this cookbook is filled with excellent meal ideas that are simple enough for the busiest of people.

We didn't just think about getting dinner together. No ma'am! We looked at the whole picture. If a meal made a big mess in our kitchen, it didn't make the cookbook. If we couldn't locate the ingredients at our local grocery store, we didn't include them. These recipes are simple from start to finish without sacrificing one bit of flavor.

After all, a few minutes saved in the kitchen are a few more minutes to spend with your family. And that is time

CONTENTS

Appetizers 7

Beverages 26

Breakfast & Brunch 35

Soups & Salads 63

Side Dishes......................... 101

Beef...................................... 127

Chicken 147

Pork 183

Seafood 203

CONTENTS

Desserts 219

U.S. Measurements 264

Grocery List 265-266

Food Substitutions.............267

Index 268-284

Cookbooks Published 286

Order Form 287

There is a time every day when the phones are quiet, TV is off and e-mails will wait until later.

For a few moments, you are not a student or an executive; at a PTA meeting or on a sales call.

For this short time, you are family.

This is dinnertime.

Bringing Family and Friends to the Table

APPETIZERS

Fiesta Dip

1 (15 ounce) can tamales	425 g
1 (16 ounce) can chili without beans	.5 kg
1 cup salsa	240 ml
1 (8 ounce) package shredded sharp cheddar cheese	227 g
1 cup finely chopped onion	240 ml

- Mash tamales with fork.

- In saucepan, combine all ingredients and heat to mix.

- Serve hot with crackers or chips.

Onion-Guacamole Dip

1 (8 ounce) carton sour cream	227 g
1 (1 ounce) packet dry onion soup mix	28 g
2 (8 ounce) cartons prepared avocado dip	2 (227 g)
2 green onions with tops, chopped	
½ teaspoon crushed dill weed	2 ml

- Mix all ingredients and chill.

- Serve with chips.

Crunchy Asparagus Dip

1 (14 ounce) can asparagus spears, drained, chopped	396 g
½ cup mayonnaise	120 ml
¼ teaspoon hot sauce	1 ml
½ cup chopped pecans	120 ml

■ Combine all ingredients in medium bowl and chill.

■ Serve with wheat crackers.

Hot Broccoli Dip

2 (16 ounce) packages cubed Mexican Velveeta® cheese	2 (.5 kg)
1 (10 ounce) can golden mushroom soup	280 g
1 (10 ounce) package frozen chopped broccoli, thawed, drained	280 g

■ In saucepan, melt cheese with soup and stir in broccoli.

■ Heat thoroughly.

■ Serve hot with chips.

Horsey Shrimp Dip

1 (8 ounce) package cream cheese, softened	227 g
⅔ cup mayonnaise	160 ml
1 tablespoon lemon juice	15 ml
3 tablespoons creamy horseradish	45 ml
¼ cup chili sauce	60 ml
½ teaspoon Creole seasoning	2 ml
¼ teaspoon garlic powder	1 ml
2 (8 ounce) cans shrimp, drained	2 (227 g)
2 green onions with tops, chopped	

- In mixing bowl, combine cream cheese, mayonnaise, lemon juice, horseradish, chili sauce, Creole seasoning and garlic powder and blend well.

- Chop shrimp and onions, add to cream cheese mixture, blend and chill. Serve with chips.

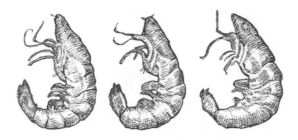

Hot Sombrero Dip

2 (15 ounce) cans bean dip	2 (425 g)
1 pound lean ground beef, cooked	.5 kg
1 (4 ounce) can green chilies	114 g
1 cup hot salsa	240 ml
1½ cups shredded Mexican Velveeta® cheese	360 ml

- Preheat oven to 350° (176° C).

- Layer bean dip, ground beef, chilies and salsa in 3-quart baking dish and top with cheese.

- Bake just until cheese melts, about 10 or 15 minutes.

- Serve with tortilla chips.

Vegetable Dip

1 (10 ounce) package frozen chopped spinach, thawed, well drained	280 g
1 bunch fresh green onions with tops, chopped	
1 (1 ounce) packet dry vegetable soup mix	28 g
1 tablespoon lemon juice	15 ml
2 (8 ounce) cartons sour cream	2 (227 g)

- Squeeze spinach in paper towels to drain thoroughly.

- In medium bowl, combine all ingredients and add a little salt. (Adding several drops of hot sauce is also good.)

- Cover and refrigerate. Serve with chips.

Velvet Clam Dip

1 (8 ounce) and 1 (3 ounce) package cream cheese	227g/84 g
¼ cup (½ stick) butter	60 ml
2 (6 ounce) cans minced clams, drained	2 (168 g)
½ teaspoon Worcestershire sauce	2 ml

- Melt cream cheese and butter in double boiler.
- Add minced clams and Worcestershire sauce.
- Serve hot.

Chunky Shrimp Dip

2 (6 ounce) cans tiny, cooked shrimp, drained	2 (168 g)
2 cups mayonnaise	480 ml
6 green onions with tops, finely chopped	
¾ cup chunky salsa	180 ml

- Crumble shrimp and stir in mayonnaise, onion and salsa.
- Chill for 1 to 2 hours.
- Serve with crackers.

Hot Rich Crab Dip

1 (10 ounce) can cheddar cheese soup	280 g
1 (16 ounce) package cubed Mexican Velveeta® cheese	.5 kg
1 (6 ounce) can crabmeat, flaked, drained	168 g
1 (16 ounce) jar salsa	.5 kg

- In microwave-safe bowl, combine soup and cheese.
- Microwave at 1-minute intervals until cheese melts.
- Add crabmeat and salsa and mix well.
- Serve hot with chips.

Unbelievable Crab Dip

Don't count on your guests leaving the table until this dip is gone!

1 (16 ounce) package cubed Velveeta® cheese	.5 kg
2 (6 ounce) cans crabmeat, drained, flaked	2 (168 g)
1 bunch fresh green onions with tops, chopped	
2 cups mayonnaise	480 ml
½ teaspoon seasoned salt	2 ml

- Melt cheese in top of double boiler. Add crabmeat, onions, mayonnaise and seasoned salt.
- Serve hot or at room temperature with assorted crackers.

Tasty Tuna Dip

1 (6 ounce) can tuna in spring water, drained, flaked	168 g
1 (1 ounce) packet dry Italian salad dressing mix	28 g
1 (8 ounce) carton sour cream	227 g
¼ cup chopped black olives, drained	60 ml

- Combine all ingredients and stir until they blend.
- Chill for 8 hours. Serve with melba rounds.

Hot Artichoke Spread

1 (14 ounce) can artichoke hearts, drained, chopped	396 g
1 (4 ounce) can chopped green chilies, drained	114 g
1 cup mayonnaise	240 ml
1 cup shredded mozzarella cheese	240 ml
¼ teaspoon white pepper	1 ml
½ teaspoon garlic salt	2 ml
Paprika	

- Preheat oven to 300° (148° C).
- Remove any spikes or tough leaves from artichoke hearts. Combine all ingredients and mix well.
- Place in sprayed 9-inch (23 cm) baking dish and sprinkle paprika over top.
- Bake for 30 minutes. Serve warm with tortilla chips or crackers.

Creamy Ham Dip

This will also make great little sandwiches on party rye bread.

2 (8 ounce) packages cream cheese, softened	2 (227 g)
2 (6 ounce) cans deviled ham	2 (168 g)
2 heaping tablespoons horseradish	30 ml
¼ cup minced onion	60 ml
¼ cup finely chopped celery	60 ml

- In mixing bowl, beat cream cheese until creamy.

- Stir in ham, horseradish, onion and celery.

- Chill and serve with crackers.

Nutty Apple Dip

1 (8 ounce) package cream cheese, softened	227 g
1 cup packed brown sugar	240 ml
1 teaspoon vanilla extract	5 ml
1 cup finely chopped pecans	240 ml

- In small mixing bowl combine cream cheese, sugar and vanilla and beat until smooth.

- Stir in pecans. Serve with sliced apples for dipping.

Zippy Broccoli-Cheese Dip

1 (10 ounce) package frozen chopped broccoli,
   thawed, drained   280 g
2 tablespoons butter   30 ml
2 ribs celery, chopped
1 small onion, finely chopped
1 (16 ounce) package cubed mild Mexican
   Velveeta® cheese   .5 kg

- Make sure broccoli is thoroughly thawed and drained.

- Place butter in large saucepan and saute broccoli, celery and onion at medium heat for about 5 minutes. Stir several times.

- Add cheese. Heat just until cheese melts and stir constantly.

- Serve hot with chips.

TIP: If you want the "zip" to be zippier, use hot Mexican Velveeta® cheese instead of mild.

Tuna Melt Appetizer

1 (10 ounce) package frozen spinach, drained   280 g
2 (6 ounce) cans white tuna in water, drained,
    flaked   2 (168 g)
¾ cup mayonnaise   180 ml
1½ cups shredded mozzarella cheese, divided   360 ml

- Preheat oven to 350° (176° C).

- Squeeze spinach in several paper towels to drain thoroughly.

- In large bowl, combine spinach, tuna, mayonnaise and 1 cup (240 ml) cheese and mix well.

- Spoon into sprayed pie pan and bake for 15 minutes.

- Remove from oven and sprinkle remaining cheese over top.

- Return to oven and bake for additional 5 minutes.

- Serve with crackers.

Hot Cocktail Squares

1 (4 ounce) can chopped green chilies	114 g
1 (3 ounce) jar bacon bits	84 g
1 (16 ounce) package shredded cheddar cheese	.5 kg
7 eggs	

- Preheat oven to 350° (176° C).

- In sprayed 7 x 11-inch (18 x 28 cm) baking dish, layer green chilies, bacon bits and cheese.

- Beat eggs well with fork and season with a little salt and several drops hot sauce. Pour over cheese and bake covered for 25 minutes.

- Uncover and bake additional 10 minutes. Cut into squares and serve warm.

Walnut-Cheese Spread

¾ cup chopped walnuts	180 ml
1 (16 ounce) package shredded cheddar cheese	.5 kg
3 fresh green onions with tops, chopped	
½ - ¾ cup mayonnaise	120 ml
½ teaspoon liquid smoke	2 ml

- Roast walnuts at 250Υ (121° C) for 10 minutes.

- Combine all ingredients and let stand in refrigerator overnight.

- Spread on assorted crackers.

Speedy Chili Con Queso

1 (16 ounce) package cubed Velveeta® cheese	.5 kg
½ cup milk	120 ml
1 (12 ounce) jar salsa, divided	340 g

- In saucepan, melt cheese and milk in double boiler.
- Add about half of salsa. Taste and add more salsa as needed for desired heat!
- Serve with tortilla chips.

Sausage-Pineapple Bits

This "sweet and hot" combination has a delicious flavor.

1 pound link sausage, cooked, skinned	.5 kg
1 pound hot bulk sausage	.5 kg
1 (15 ounce) can crushed pineapple with juice	425 g
2 cups packed brown sugar	480 ml
1 tablespoon white wine Worcestershire sauce	15 ml

- Slice link sausage into ⅓-inch (.8 cm) pieces. Shape bulk sausage into 1-inch (2.5 cm) balls.
- In skillet, brown sausage balls.
- In large saucepan, combine pineapple, brown sugar and Worcestershire. Heat, add both sausages and simmer for 30 minutes.
- Serve from chafing dish or small slow cooker with cocktail toothpicks.

Party Smokies

1 cup ketchup	240 ml
1 cup plum jelly	240 ml
1 tablespoon lemon juice	15 ml
4 tablespoons mustard	60 ml
2 (5 ounce) packages tiny smoked sausages	2 (143 g)

- In saucepan, combine ketchup, jelly, lemon juice and mustard, heat and mix well.

- Add sausages and simmer for 10 minutes.

- Serve hot with cocktail toothpicks.

Sausage Bites

1 (1 pound) package hot sausage	.5 kg
1 (16 ounce) package shredded colby or cheddar cheese	.5 kg
3¾ cups biscuit mix	890 ml
½ teaspoon garlic powder	2 ml

- Preheat oven to 350° (176° C).

- Combine all ingredients and knead thoroughly.

- Roll into 1-inch (2.5 cm) balls.

- Bake on baking sheet for 15 to 18 minutes or until light brown.

Spinach-Artichoke Dip

2 (10 ounce) packages frozen spinach, thawed, drained	2 (280 g)
1 (14 ounce) jar marinated artichoke hearts, drained, finely chopped	396 g
1 cup mayonnaise	240 ml
2 cups shredded mozzarella cheese	480 ml

- Squeeze spinach in paper towels to drain thoroughly.
- Combine all ingredients and mix well.
- Cover and chill.
- Serve with chips.

Olive-Cheese Balls

2¼ cups shredded sharp cheddar cheese	540 ml
1 cup flour	240 ml
½ cup (1 stick) butter, melted	120 ml
1 (5 ounce) jar green olives	143 g

- Preheat oven to 350° (176° C).
- In large bowl, combine cheese and flour. Add butter and mix well.
- Cover olives with mixture and form into balls.
- Bake for about 15 minutes or until light brown.

Creamy Spinach-Pepper Dip

1 (10 ounce) package frozen chopped spinach, drained	280 g
1 (8 ounce) package shredded Monterey Jack cheese	227 g
1 (8 ounce) package cream cheese, softened	227 g
1 - 2 tablespoons chopped jalapenos	15 ml

- Drain spinach several times, wrap in paper towels and squeeze remaining liquid from spinach.

- Combine spinach, Monterey Jack, cream cheese and jalapenos in microwave-safe bowl and heat in microwave on MEDIUM until cheese melts. Stir several times while heating.

- Serve hot with chips or crackers.

To quickly slice mushrooms, small tomatoes, radishes and similar firm fruits and vegetables, use an egg slicer.

Creamy Onion Dip

2 (8 ounce) packages cream cheese, softened	2 (227 g)
3 tablespoons lemon juice	45 ml
1 (1 ounce) packet dry onion soup mix	28 g
1 (8 ounce) carton sour cream	227 g

- Use mixer to beat cream cheese until smooth.

- Add lemon juice and soup mix. Gradually fold in sour cream and blend well.

- Chill and serve with chips, crackers or fresh vegetables.

Favorite Stand-By Shrimp Dip

2 cups tiny, cooked shrimp, finely chopped	480 ml
2 tablespoons horseradish	30 ml
½ cup chili sauce	120 ml
¾ cup mayonnaise	180 ml
1 tablespoon lemon juice	15 ml

- Combine all ingredients with a few dashes salt and refrigerate. (If shrimp has been frozen, be sure to drain well.)

- Serve with cucumber or zucchini slices.

Crab Dip Kick

1 (8 ounce) package cream cheese, softened	227 g
3 tablespoons salsa	45 ml
2 tablespoons horseradish	30 ml
1 (6 ounce) can crabmeat, drained, flaked	168 g

- In mixing bowl, beat cream cheese until creamy.

- Add salsa and horseradish and mix well.

- Stir in crabmeat and refrigerate.

- Serve with assorted crackers.

Creamy Cucumber Spread

1 (8 ounce) package cream cheese, softened	227 g
½ cup mayonnaise	120 ml
1 teaspoon seasoned salt	5 ml
1 cup seeded, chopped cucumbers	240 ml

- With mixer, beat cream cheese until creamy and add mayonnaise, seasoned salt and cucumber.

- Spread on crackers.

Reuse those holiday tins. Once the cookies are all gone, use these colorful tins to store baking items and accessories, such as all those tools you used to decorate that cake - five years ago.

Roasted Garlic Dip

4 - 5 whole garlic cloves with peel
2 (8 ounce) packages cream cheese, softened   2 (227 g)
¾ cup mayonnaise   180 ml
1 (7 or 9 ounce) jar roasted sweet red peppers,
    drained, coarsely chopped   198 g
1 bunch fresh green onions with tops, chopped

- Preheat oven to 400° (204° C).

- Lightly brush outside of garlic cloves with a little oil and place in shallow baking pan.

- Heat about 10 minutes and cool.

- Press roasted garlic out of cloves.

- Beat cream cheese and mayonnaise until creamy. Add garlic, red peppers and onions and mix well. (Roasted peppers are great in this recipe, but if you want it a little spicy, add several drops of hot sauce.)

- Sprinkle with red pepper or paprika and serve with chips.

Cranberry-Pineapple Punch

1 (48 ounce) bottle cranberry juice	1.3 kg
1 (46 ounce) can pineapple juice	1.3 kg
½ cup sugar	120 ml
2 teaspoons almond extract	10 ml
1 (2 liter) bottle ginger ale, chilled	2 L

- Combine cranberry juice, pineapple juice, sugar and almond extract and stir until sugar dissolves. Cover and chill 8 hours.

- When ready to serve, add ginger ale and stir.

Best Tropical Punch

1 (46 ounce) can pineapple juice	1.3 kg
1 (46 ounce) can apricot nectar	1.3 kg
3 (6 ounce) cans frozen limeade concentrate, thawed	3 (168 g)
1 (3 quart) ginger ale, chilled	3 L

- Combine pineapple juice, apricot nectar and limeade concentrate and chill.

- When ready to serve, add ginger ale.

Champagne Punch

1 (750 ml) bottle champagne, chilled
1 (32 ounce) bottle ginger ale, chilled   1 kg
1 (6 ounce) can frozen orange juice concentrate   168 g
Orange slices, optional

- Combine champagne, ginger ale and orange juice concentrate in punch bowl and mix well.

- Serve chilled and garnish with orange slices.

Orange Slush

2 cups orange juice   480 ml
½ cup instant, non-fat dry milk   120 ml
¼ teaspoon almond extract   1 ml
8 ice cubes

- Combine all ingredients in blender and process on high until mixture is smooth and thick.

- Serve immediately.

If you need a quick festive punch or a special, celebratory drink, champagne and canned fruit juices can save the day. Choose tropical flavors or bright colors. Mix two parts champagne and one or two parts juice and you have a beautiful, delightful drink in just a few minutes.

Lemon-Banana Shake

1 (6 ounce) can frozen lemonade concentrate, thawed	168 g
1 cup diced bananas	240 ml
1 (1 quart) vanilla ice cream	1 L
3 cups milk	710 ml

- In mixing bowl, combine lemonade concentrate and bananas and beat until mixture is thick.

- For each milkshake, add 1 scoop vanilla ice cream and ¼ cup (60 ml) lemon-banana mixture in glass.

- Fill glass two-thirds full with milk and stir well.

- Top off with 1 more scoop of ice cream.

Hot Cranberry Cider

1½ quarts cranberry juice	1.5 L
1 (12 ounce) can frozen orange juice concentrate, thawed	340 g
½ teaspoon cinnamon	2 ml

- Combine cranberry juice, orange juice and 1½ orange juice cans water in large saucepan. Bring to a boil to blend flavors.

- Add cinnamon and stir well.

- Serve hot.

Very Special Coffee Punch

I Promise – This Will Make a Hit!

1 (2 ounce) jar instant coffee	57 g
2¼ cups sugar	540 ml
2 quarts half-and-half cream	2 L
1 (1 quart) ginger ale	1 L
1 (1 pint) whipping cream, whipped	.5 kg
½ gallon French vanilla ice cream	2 L

- Dissolve instant coffee in 2 quarts (2 L) hot water and cool. Add sugar and half-and-half, mix well and chill.

- When ready to serve, pour coffee-sugar mixture in punch bowl, add chilled ginger ale, whipped cream and ice cream. Let some chunks of ice cream remain.

- This will make 60 (4 ounce/114 g) servings.

- *Everyone will be back for seconds!*

Mexican Coffee

1 ounce Kahlua®	28 g
1 cup hot, black coffee	240 ml
Ground cinnamon	
Sweetened whipped cream	

- Pour Kahlua® and coffee into tall mug.

- Sprinkle with cinnamon and stir. Top with whipped cream.

Holiday Party Punch

The almond extract really gives this punch a special taste!

3 cups sugar	710 ml
1 (6 ounce) package lemon gelatin	168 g
1 (3 ounce) can frozen orange juice concentrate,	
thawed	84 g
⅓ cup lemon juice	80 ml
1 (46 ounce) can pineapple juice	1.3 kg
3 tablespoons almond extract	45 ml
2 quarts ginger ale, chilled	2 L

- Combine sugar and 1-quart (1 L) water. Heat until sugar dissolves.

- Add gelatin and stir until it dissolves. Add fruit juices, 1½ quarts (1.5 L) water and almond extract and chill.

- When ready to serve, place in punch bowl and add chilled ginger ale.

- This will make 50 servings.

Green Party Punch

This punch would be great for St. Patrick's Day!

1 (3 ounce) package lime gelatin	84 g
1 (6 ounce) can frozen limeade, thawed	168 g
1 (6 ounce) can frozen lemonade, thawed	168 g
1 (1 quart) orange juice	1 L
1 (1 quart) pineapple juice	1 L
1 tablespoon almond extract	15 ml
2 - 3 drops green food coloring	
1 (1 liter) ginger ale, chilled	1 L

- Dissolve lime gelatin and 1 cup (240 ml) boiling water and stir well.

- In 1-gallon (1 L) bottle, combine dissolved gelatin, limeade, lemonade, orange juice, pineapple juice, almond extract and food coloring and chill.

- When ready to serve, add ginger ale.

- Serves 32.

Reception Punch

4 cups sugar	1 L
5 ripe bananas, mashed	
Juice of 2 lemons	
1 (46 ounce) can pineapple juice	1.3 kg
1 (6 once) can frozen undiluted orange juice,	
thawed	168 g
2 quarts ginger ale	2 L

- Boil sugar and 6 cups (1.5 L) water for 3 minutes and cool.

- Blend bananas with lemon juice and add pineapple and orange juice.

- Combine all ingredients except ginger ale. Freeze in large container.

- To serve, thaw 1½ hours, then add ginger ale. Punch will be slushy.

- Serves 40.

Strawberry Punch

2 (10 ounce) boxes frozen strawberries,
   thawed   2 (280 g)
2 (6 ounce) cans frozen pink lemonade
   concentrate   2 (168 g)
2 (2 liter) bottles ginger ale, chilled   2 (2 L)

- Process strawberries through blender. Pour lemonade into punch bowl and stir in strawberries.

- Add chilled ginger ale and stir well. (It would be nice to make an ice ring out of another bottle of ginger ale.)

Sparkling Punch

6 oranges, unpeeled, thinly sliced
1 cup sugar   240 ml
2 bottles dry white wine
3 bottles sparkling wine, chilled

- Place orange slices in large plastic or glass container and sprinkle with sugar.

- Add white wine, cover and chill at least 8 hours.

- Stir in sparkling wine.

Strawberry Smoothie

2 medium bananas, peeled, sliced	
1 pint fresh strawberries, washed, quartered	.5 kg
1 (8 ounce) container strawberry yogurt	227 g
¼ cup orange juice	60 ml

- Place all ingredients in blender. Process until smooth.
- Serve as is or over crushed ice.

Banana-Mango Smoothie

1 cup peeled, cubed ripe mango	240 ml
1 ripe banana, sliced	
⅔ cup milk	160 ml
1 teaspoon honey	5 ml
¼ teaspoon vanilla extract	1 ml

- Arrange mango cubes in single layer on baking sheet and freeze about 1 hour or until firm.
- Combine frozen mango, banana, milk, honey and vanilla and pour into blender.
- Process until smooth.

BREAKFAST
& BRUNCH

Breakfast Bake

This is a favorite for overnight guests and even special enough for Christmas morning.

1 pound hot sausage, cooked, crumbled	.5 kg
1 cup shredded cheddar cheese	240 ml
1 cup biscuit mix	240 ml
5 eggs, slightly beaten	
2 cups milk	240 ml

- Preheat oven to 350° (176° C).

- Place sausage in sprayed 9 x 13-inch (23 x 33 cm) baking dish and sprinkle with cheese.

- In mixing bowl, combine biscuit mix, eggs and a little salt and beat well.

- Add milk to egg mixture and stir until fairly smooth. Pour over sausage mixture.

- Bake for 35 minutes. (You can mix this up the night before cooking and refrigerate. To cook the next morning, add 5 minutes to cooking time.)

Breakfast Tacos

4 eggs
4 flour tortillas
1 cup cooked, chopped ham   240 ml
1 cup shredded cheddar cheese   240 ml

- Scramble eggs in skillet.

- Lay tortillas flat and spoon eggs over 4 tortillas.

- Sprinkle with ham and cheese and roll to enclose filling.

- Place tacos in microwave-safe dish and microwave for 30 seconds or until cheese melts.

- Serve immediately.

Bacon-Egg Burrito

2 slices bacon, cooked, chopped
2 eggs, scrambled
¼ cup shredded cheddar cheese   60 ml
1 flour tortilla

- Sprinkle bacon, eggs and cheese in middle of tortilla. (Add taco sauce or salsa if you like.)
- Fold tortilla sides over and place seam-side down on dinner plate.
- Microwave for 30 seconds or just until mixture heats thoroughly.

Glazed Bacon

1 (1 pound) bacon   .5 kg
⅓ cup packed brown sugar   80 ml
1 teaspoon flour   5 ml
½ cup finely chopped pecans   120 ml

- Preheat oven to 350° (176° C).
- Arrange bacon slices close together, but not overlapping, on wire rack over drip pan.
- In bowl, combine brown sugar, flour and pecans and sprinkle evenly over bacon.
- Bake for 30 minutes. Drain on paper towels.

Curried Fruit Medley

1 (29 ounce) can sliced peaches	805 g
2 (15 ounce) cans pineapple chunks	2 (425 g)
1 (10 ounce) jar maraschino cherries	280 g
1 cup packed brown sugar	240 ml
1 teaspoon curry powder	5 ml
¼ cup (½ stick) butter, cut into pieces	60 ml

- Preheat oven to 350° (176° C).

- Drain all fruit and place in 9 x 13-inch (23 x 33 cm) baking dish. Combine brown sugar and curry and stir well. Sprinkle over fruit and dot with butter.

- Bake covered for 30 minutes or until thoroughly hot.

Apricot Bake

4 (15 ounce) cans apricot halves, drained divided	4 (425 g)
1 (16 ounce) box light brown sugar, divided	.5 kg
2 cups round, buttery cracker crumbs, divided	480 ml
½ cup (1 stick) butter, sliced	120 ml

- Preheat oven to 300° (148° C). Spray 9 x 13-inch (23 x 33 cm) baking dish and line with 2 cans drained apricots.

- Sprinkle half brown sugar and half cracker crumbs over apricots. Dot with half butter and repeat layers.

- Bake for 1 hour.

Pineapple-Cheese Casserole

*This is really a different kind of recipe and very good. It can be
served at brunch and is also great with sandwiches at lunch.*

1 cup sugar	240 ml
5 tablespoons flour	75 ml
2 (20 ounce) cans unsweetened pineapple chunks, drained	2 (567 g)
1½ cups shredded cheddar cheese	360 ml
1 stack round, buttery crackers, crushed	
½ cup (1 stick) butter, melted	120 ml

- Preheat oven to 350° (176° C).

- Combine sugar and flour.

- Spray 9 x 13-inch (23 x 33 cm) baking dish and layer pineapple, sugar-flour mixture, grated cheese and cracker crumbs (in that order).

- Drizzle butter over casserole.

- Bake for 25 minutes or until bubbly.

Ranch Sausage-Grits

1 cup quick-cooking grits	240 ml
1 (1 pound) pork sausage	.5 kg
1 onion, chopped	
1 cup salsa	240 ml
1 (8 ounce) package shredded cheddar cheese, divided	227 g

- Preheat oven to 350° (176° C).

- Cook grits according to package directions and set aside.

- Cook and brown sausage and onion and drain well.

- Combine grits, sausage mixture, salsa and half of cheese and spoon into sprayed 2-quart (2 L) baking dish.

- Bake for 15 minutes.

- Remove from oven, add remaining cheese and bake additional 10 minutes.

- Serve hot.

This is a great dish for a Sunday night breakfast, Start a fun family tradition with breakfast on Sunday Nights.

Cinnamon Souffle

1 loaf cinnamon-raisin bread
1 (20 ounce) can crushed pineapple with juice   567 g
1 cup (2 sticks) butter, melted   240 ml
½ cup sugar   120 ml
5 eggs, slightly beaten

- Preheat oven to 350° (176° C).

- Slice very thin portion of bread crusts off.

- Tear bread into small pieces and place in sprayed 9 x 13-inch (23 x 33 cm) baking dish.

- Pour pineapple and juice over bread and set aside.

- Cream butter and sugar.

- Add eggs to creamed mixture and mix well.

- Pour creamed mixture over bread and pineapple. Bake uncovered for 40 minutes.

TIP: If you have some pecans handy, ½ cup chopped pecans really adds extra texture and flavor.

Mexican Breakfast Eggs

¼ cup (½ stick) butter   60 ml
9 eggs
3 tablespoons milk   45 ml
5 tablespoons salsa   75 ml
1 cup crushed tortilla chips   240 ml

- Melt butter in skillet.

- In bowl, beat eggs and add milk and salsa.

- Pour egg mixture into skillet and stir until eggs cook lightly.

- Stir in tortilla chips and serve hot.

Light, Crispy Waffles

2 cups biscuit mix   480 ml
1 egg
½ cup oil   120 ml
1⅓ cups club soda   320 ml

- Preheat waffle iron.

- Combine all ingredients in mixing bowl and stir by hand. Pour just enough batter to cover waffle iron and cook.

TIP: To have waffles for a "company weekend", make them before the guests arrive. Freeze the waffles separately on a baking sheet and place in large plastic bags. To heat, bake at 350° (176° C) for about 10 minutes.

Bacon-Sour Cream Omelet

2 eggs
5 strips bacon, fried, drained, crumbled
⅓ cup sour cream   80 ml
3 green onions, chopped
1 tablespoon butter   15 ml

- Use fork to beat eggs with 1 tablespoon (15 ml) water. Combine bacon and sour cream. Saute onions in bacon drippings and mix with bacon-sour cream.

- Melt butter in omelet pan. Pour in egg mixture and cook. When omelet is set, spoon sour cream mixture along center and fold omelet onto warm plate.

Pineapple Coffee Cake

1 (18 ounce) box butter cake mix   510 g
½ cup oil   120 ml
4 eggs, slightly beaten
1 (20 ounce) can pineapple pie filling   567 g

- Preheat oven to 350° (176° C). In mixing bowl combine mix, oil and eggs and beat well. Pour batter into sprayed, floured 9 x 13-inch (23 x 33 cm) baking pan.

- Bake for 45 to 50 minutes. Cake is done when toothpick inserted in center comes out clean

- Punch holes in cake about 2 inches (5 cm) apart with knife. Spread pineapple pie filling over cake while hot.

Cranberry Coffee Cake

2 eggs
1 cup mayonnaise   240 ml
1 (18 ounce) box spice cake mix   510 ml
1 (16 ounce) can whole cranberry sauce   .5 kg
Powdered sugar

- Preheat oven to 325° (162° C).

- Beat together eggs, mayonnaise and cake mix with mixer and fold in cranberry sauce.

- Pour into sprayed, floured 9 x 13-inch (23 x 33 cm) baking pan.

- Bake for 45 minutes. Cake is done when toothpick inserted in center comes out clean.

- When cake is cool, dust with powdered sugar. (If you would rather have icing than powdered sugar, use prepared icing.)

Pecan Waffles

2 cups flour	480 ml
½ cup oil	120 ml
½ cup milk	120 ml
⅔ cup finely chopped pecans	160 ml

- Preheat waffle iron.

- In bowl, combine flour, oil and milk and mix well.

- Stir in chopped pecans.

- Pour approximately ¾ cup (180 ml) batter onto hot waffle iron and cook until brown and crispy.

Christmas Breakfast

12 - 14 eggs, slightly beaten	
1 pound sausage, cooked, drained, crumbled	.5 kg
2 cups whole milk	480 ml
1½ cups shredded cheddar cheese	360 ml
1 (5 ounce) box seasoned croutons	143 g

- Preheat oven to 350° (176° C).

- Mix all ingredients and pour into 9 x 13-inch (23 x 33 cm) baking dish.

- Bake for 40 minutes.

- Let rest for about 10 minutes before serving.

Homemade Egg Substitute

6 egg whites	
¼ cup instant nonfat dry milk powder	60 m
2 teaspoons oil	10 ml
¼ teaspoon ground turmeric	1 ml

- Combine all ingredients in blender, add 2 teaspoons (10 ml) water and process 30 seconds.

- Refrigerate.

Green Chile Squares

2 cups chopped green chilies	480 ml
1 (8 ounce) package shredded sharp cheddar cheese	227 g
8 eggs, beaten	
½ cup half-and-half cream	120 ml

- Preheat oven to 350° (176° C).

- Place green chilies in bottom of 9 x 13-inch (23 x 33 cm) baking pan and cover with cheese.

- Combine eggs, a little salt and pepper and half-and-half and pour over chilies and cheese.

- Bake for 30 minutes.

- Let rest at room temperature for a few minutes before cutting into squares.

Baked Grits

2 cups quick-cooking grits	480 ml
2 cups milk	480 ml
¾ cup (1½ sticks) butter	180 ml
4 eggs, beaten	

- Preheat oven to 350° (176° C).

- Stir grits in 4 cups (1 L) water over medium heat for about 5 minutes.

- Add milk and butter, cover and cook additional 10 minutes.

- Remove from heat and add eggs.

- Pour in sprayed baking dish and bake for 30 minutes.

Praline Toast

½ cup (1 stick) butter, softened	120 ml
1 cup packed brown sugar	120 ml
½ cup finely chopped pecans	120 ml
Bread slices	

- Combine butter, brown sugar and pecans and mix well.

- Spread butter mixture on bread slices.

- Toast in broiler until brown and bubbly.

Peach Bake

2 (15 ounce) cans peach halves, drained	2 (425 g)
1 cup packed brown sugar	240 ml
1 cup round, buttery cracker crumbs	240 ml
½ cup (1 stick) butter, melted	120 ml

- Preheat oven to 325° (162° C).

- Spray 2-quart (2 L) baking dish and layer peaches, sugar and cracker crumbs until all ingredients are used. Pour melted butter over casserole.

- Bake for 35 minutes or until cracker crumbs are slightly brown. Serve hot or at room temperature.

Sour Cream Biscuits

2 cups plus 1 tablespoon flour	480 ml/15 ml
3 teaspoons baking powder	15 ml
½ teaspoon baking soda	2 ml
½ cup shortening	120 ml
1 (8 ounce) carton sour cream	227 g

- Preheat oven to 400° (204° C). Combine dry ingredients, add a little salt and cut in shortening.

- Gradually add sour cream and mix lightly. Turn on lightly floured board and knead a few times. Roll to ½-inch (1.2 cm) thickness. Cut with biscuit cutter and place on sprayed baking sheet.

- Bake for 15 minutes or until light brown.

Cheesy Herb Bread

1 loaf French bread	
½ teaspoon garlic powder	2 ml
1 teaspoon marjoram leaves	5 ml
1 tablespoon dried parsley leaves	15 ml
½ cup (1 stick) butter, softened	120 ml
1 cup parmesan cheese	240 ml

- Preheat oven to 375° (190° C).

- Slice bread into 1-inch (2.5 cm) slices. Combine garlic, marjoram, parsley and butter. Spread mixture on bread slices and sprinkle with cheese.

- Wrap in foil and bake for 20 minutes. Unwrap and bake additional 5 minutes.

Garlic Toast

1 loaf French bread	
1 tablespoon garlic powder	15 ml
2 tablespoons dried parsley flakes	30 ml
½ cup (1 stick) butter, melted	120 ml
1 cup parmesan cheese	240 ml

- Preheat oven to 225° (107° C).

- Slice bread diagonally into 1-inch (2.5 cm) slices. Combine ingredients, except cheese, in small bowl and mix well. Brush mixture on bread and sprinkle cheese.

- Place on baking sheet and bake for about 1 hour.

Popovers

2 cups flour   480 ml
6 eggs, beaten
2 cups milk   480 ml
Butter

- Preheat oven to 425° (220° C).

- Combine flour and 1 teaspoon (5 ml) salt in bowl. Add eggs and milk and mix. Add dry ingredients and mix well. (The batter will be like heavy cream.)

- Coat popover pans with butter and heat in oven. Fill each cup half full. Bake for 20 minutes. Reduce heat to 375Υ (190° C) and bake additional 25 minutes. Serve immediately.

Salad Muffins

⅓ cup sugar   80 ml
⅓ cup oil   80 ml
¾ cup milk   180 ml
2 eggs
2 cups biscuit mix   480 ml

- Preheat oven to 400° (204° C).

- In mixing bowl, combine sugar, oil and milk. Beat in eggs and biscuit mix. Mix well; mixture will be a little lumpy. Pour into sprayed muffin pans two-thirds full.

- Bake for about 10 minutes or until light brown.

Spicy Cornbread Twists

3 tablespoons butter	45 ml
⅓ cup cornmeal	80 ml
¼ teaspoon red pepper	1 ml
1 (11 ounce) can refrigerated soft breadsticks	312 g

- Preheat oven to 350° (176° C).

- Place butter in pie plate and melt in oven. Remove from oven.

- On wax paper, mix cornmeal and red pepper. Roll breadsticks in butter and cornmeal mixture.

- Twist breadsticks according to package directions and place on baking sheet. Bake for 15 to 18 minutes.

Souper-Sausage Cornbread

1 (10 ounce) can golden corn soup	280 g
2 eggs	
¼ cup milk	60 ml
2 (16 ounce) package corn muffin mix	2 (.5 kg)
¼ pound pork sausage, cooked, drained, crumbled	114 g

- Preheat oven to 400° (204° C).

- In bowl, combine soup, eggs and milk. Stir in muffin mix just until blended. Fold in sausage. Spoon mixture into sprayed 9 x 13-inch (23 x 33 cm) baking pan.

- Bake for about 20 minutes or until light brown.

Cream Biscuits

2 cups flour	480 ml
3 teaspoons baking powder	15 ml
1 (8 ounce) carton whipping cream	227 g

- Preheat oven to 375° (190° C).

- Combine flour, baking powder and ½ teaspoon (2 ml) salt. In mixing bowl, beat whipping cream only until it holds a shape. Combine flour mixture and cream and mix with fork.

- Put dough on lightly floured board and knead about 1 minute. Pat dough to ¾-inch (1.8 cm) thickness. Cut biscuits with small biscuit cutter.

- Bake on baking sheet for about 12 minutes or until light brown.

Orange French Toast

1 egg, beaten	
½ cup orange juice	120 ml
5 slices raisin bread	
1 cup crushed graham crackers	240 ml
2 tablespoons butter	30 ml

- Combine egg and orange juice. Dip bread in mixture and then in crumbs.

- Fry in butter until brown.

Strawberry Bread

Great for finger food at parties or as sandwiches with cream cheese and pecans and red is always "in"!

3 cups flour	710 ml
1 teaspoon baking soda	5 ml
1 teaspoon cinnamon	5 ml
2 cups sugar	480 ml
2 (10 ounce) cartons frozen strawberries, thawed	2 (280 g)
1¼ cups oil	300 ml
4 eggs, beaten	
1 teaspoon red food coloring	5 ml

- Preheat oven to 350° (176° C).

- Combine flour, baking soda, cinnamon, ½ teaspoon (2 ml) salt and sugar in mixing bowl.

- With spoon, make a "well" in dry ingredients, add strawberries, oil and eggs and mix well. Add food coloring and mix well.

- Pour into 2 sprayed, floured loaf pans.

- Bake for 1 hour.

You can save some time by slicing or chopping vegetables all at one time, then storing them in plastic bags in the refrigerator. When you're ready to use them, just pull out the bag and use what you need. You'd be surprised how nice it is.

Caramel Rolls

9 tablespoons butter, softened, divided	115 ml
1 cup packed light brown sugar	240 ml
½ cup chopped pecans	120 ml
2 (8 ounce) cans refrigerated crescent dinner rolls	2 (227 g)
¼ cup sugar	60 ml
2 teaspoons cinnamon	10 ml

- Preheat oven to 375° (190° C).

- In unsprayed 9 x 13-inch (23 x 33 cm) pan, melt 5 tablespoons (75 ml) butter in oven. Stir in brown sugar, ¼ cup (60 ml) water and pecans and set aside.

- Separate each can of roll dough in 4 rectangles. Pinch perforations together to seal.

- Spread with 4 tablespoons (60 ml) softened butter. Combine sugar and cinnamon and sprinkle over dough.

- Starting at shorter side, roll each rectangle and cut each roll into 4 slices, making 32 pieces. Place in prepared pan.

- Bake for 20 to 25 minutes or until golden brown. Invert immediately to remove from pan and serve warm.

Apricot-Pineapple Muffins

⅓ cup very finely cut dried apricots	80 ml
½ cup (1 stick) butter, softened	120 ml
1 cup sugar	240 ml
1 egg	
1 (8 ounce) can crushed pineapple with juice	227 g
1¼ cups flour	300 ml
½ teaspoon baking soda	2 ml
1 cup quick-rolled oats	240 ml

■ Preheat oven to 350° (176° C). With mixer, cream butter and sugar, add egg and pineapple and beat well. Add all dry ingredients and ½ teaspoon (2 ml) salt, mix well and fold in apricots.

■ Spoon into well sprayed muffin cups or use the paper liners. Bake for 20 minutes. Makes 12 muffins.

French Onion Biscuits

2 cups biscuit mix	480 ml
¼ cup milk	60 ml
1 (8 ounce) container French onion dip	227 g
2 tablespoons finely minced green onion	30 ml

■ Preheat oven to 400° (204° C).

■ Mix all ingredients until soft dough forms.

■ Drop dough by teaspoonfuls onto sprayed baking sheet. Bake for 10 minutes or until light brown.

Eagle Yeast Bread

8 cups sifted flour, divided	1.8 L
1 tablespoon sugar	15 ml
2 yeast cakes	
1 (14 ounce) can sweetened condensed milk	396 g
⅓ cup oil	80 ml

- Combine 6 cups flour, sugar and 1 tablespoon (15 ml) salt and set aside.

- Soften yeast in small amount of warm water. Add sweetened condensed milk, oil and enough warm water to measure 4 cups (1 L) and mix well.

- Add to flour mixture and mix well. Add remaining 2 cups (480 ml) flour and mix well.

- Knead 10 minutes. Place in sprayed bowl and turn out onto sprayed surface.

- Let rise, covered, for 1½ to 2 hours or until doubled in size.

- Divide into 3 portions. Place in 3 sprayed loaf pans. Let rise 40 minutes.

- Preheat oven to 350° (176° C).

- Bake approximately 40 minutes. Brush with melted butter.

Cheese Drops

2 cups biscuit mix	480 ml
⅔ cup milk	160 ml
⅔ cup shredded sharp cheddar cheese	160 ml
¼ cup (½ stick) butter, melted	60 ml

- Preheat oven to 400° (204° C).

- Combine biscuit mix, milk and cheese. Drop 1 heaping tablespoon (15 ml) dough onto sprayed baking sheet for each biscuit. Bake for 10 minutes or until light brown.

- While warm, brush tops of biscuits with melted butter. Serve hot.

Bacon-Cheese French Bread

1 (16 ounce) loaf unsliced French bread	.5 kg
5 slices bacon, cooked, crumbled	
1 (8 ounce) package shredded mozzarella cheese	227 g
½ cup (1 stick) butter, melted	120 ml

- Preheat oven to 350° (176° C).

- Slice bread into 1-inch (2.5 cm) slices and place sliced loaf on large piece aluminum foil.

- Combine bacon and cheese and sprinkle between slices of bread. Drizzle butter over loaf and let some drip in-between slices.

- Wrap loaf tightly in foil. Bake for 20 minutes or until thoroughly hot. Serve hot.

Crunchy Breadsticks

1 (8 count) package hot dog buns
1 cup (2 sticks) butter, melted   240 ml
Garlic powder
Paprika

- Preheat oven to 225° (107° C).

- Take each half bun and slice in half lengthwise.

- Use pastry brush to butter all breadsticks. Sprinkle each breadstick lightly with garlic powder and paprika. Place on baking sheet and bake for 45 minutes.

Maple Syrup Biscuits

2¼ cups biscuit mix   540 ml
⅔ cup milk   160 ml
1½ cups maple syrup   360 ml

- Preheat oven to 425° (220° C). Combine biscuit mix and milk and stir until moist. On floured surface, roll dough to ½-inch (1.2 cm) thickness. Cut out biscuits with 2-inch (5 cm) biscuit cutter.

- Pour syrup into 7 x 11-inch (18 x 28 cm) baking dish. Place biscuits on top of syrup. Bake for 13 to 15 minutes or until biscuits are golden brown.

Mozzarella Loaf

1 (16 ounce) loaf unsliced French bread	.5 kg
12 slices mozzarella cheese	
¼ cup grated parmesan cheese	60 ml
6 tablespoons (¾ stick) butter, softened	90 ml
½ teaspoon garlic salt	2 ml

- Preheat oven to 375° (190° C).

- Cut loaf into 1-inch (2.5 cm) thick slices. Place mozzarella slices between bread slices. Combine parmesan cheese, butter and garlic salt and spread on bread slices.

- Reshape loaf, press together and brush remaining butter mixture on outside of loaf. Bake 8 to 10 minutes.

Cheddar Cornbread

2 (8.5 ounce) packages cornbread muffin mix	2 (227 g)
2 eggs, beaten	
½ cup milk	120 ml
½ cup plain yogurt	120 ml
1 (14 ounce) can cream-style corn	396 g
½ cup shredded cheddar cheese	120 ml

- Preheat oven to 400° (204° C).

- In bowl, combine cornbread mix, eggs, milk and yogurt until they blend. Stir in corn and cheese and pour into sprayed 9 x 13-inch (23 x 33 cm) baking dish.

- Bake for 18 to 20 minutes or until light brown.

Raspberry-Filled Blueberry Muffins

1 (16 ounce) box blueberry muffin mix with blueberries	.5 kg
1 egg	
⅓ cup red raspberry jam	80 ml
¼ cup sliced almonds	60 ml

- Preheat oven to 375° (190° C).

- Rinse blueberries and drain.

- In bowl, combine muffin mix, egg and ½ cup (120 ml) water. Stir until moist and break up any lumps in mix.

- Place paper liners in 8 muffin cups. Fill cups half full with batter. Combine raspberry jam with blueberries and spoon mixture over batter.

- Cover with remaining batter and sprinkle almonds over batter. Bake for 18 minutes or until light brown.

Ham-Cheese Bars

2 cups biscuit mix	480 ml
1 heaping cup cooked, finely chopped ham	240 ml
1 cup shredded cheddar cheese	240 ml
½ onion, finely chopped	
½ cup grated parmesan cheese	120 ml
¼ cup sour cream	60 ml
1 teaspoon garlic powder	5 ml
1 cup whole milk	240 ml
1 egg	

- Preheat oven to 350° (176° C).

- Combine all ingredients plus ½ teaspoon (2 ml) salt in mixing bowl and mix by hand.

- Spread in sprayed 9 x 13-inch (23 x 33 cm) baking pan. Bake for 30 minutes or until light brown.

- Cut in rectangles, about 2 x 1-inch (2 x 2.5 cm). Serve hot or room temperature.

TIP: This is not exactly a casserole, but it goes well with a lot of our brunch casseroles. They can be served at brunch or lunch and they can be kept in the refrigerator (cooked) and reheated. To reheat, place in a 325° (162° C) oven for about 15 minutes. They will be good and crispy when reheated.

SOUPS
& SALADS

Broccoli-Wild Rice Soup

This is a hardy and delicious soup that is full of flavor.

1 (6 ounce) package chicken-flavored wild rice mix	168
1 (10 ounce) package frozen chopped broccoli, thawed	280 g
2 teaspoons dried minced onion	10 ml
1 (10 ounce) can cream of chicken soup	280 g
1 (8 ounce) package cream cheese, cubed	227 g

- In large saucepan, combine rice, rice seasoning packet and 6 cups water.

- Boil, reduce heat, cover and simmer for 10 minutes, stir once. Stir in broccoli and onion and simmer 5 minutes.

- Stir in soup and cream cheese. Cook and stir until cheese melts.

Navy Bean Soup

3 (16 ounce) cans navy beans with liquid	3 (.5 kg)
1 (14 ounce) can chicken broth	396 g
1 cup chopped ham	240 ml
1 large onion, chopped	
½ teaspoon garlic powder	2 ml

- In large saucepan, combine all ingredients, add 1 cup (240 ml) water and bring to a boil.

- Simmer until onion is tender-crisp and serve hot with cornbread.

Cream of Zucchini Soup

1 pound fresh zucchini, grated	.5 kg
1 onion, chopped	
1 (14 ounce) can chicken broth	396 g
½ teaspoon sweet basil	2 ml
2 cups half-and-half cream, divided	480 ml

- In saucepan, combine zucchini, onion, broth, basil and a little salt and pepper.

- Bring to a boil, simmer until soft, pour into food processor and puree.

- Gradually add ½ cup (120 ml) half-and-half and blend. (You could add ¼ teaspoon/1 ml curry powder, if you like curry flavor.)

- Return zucchini mixture to saucepan and add remaining cream. Heat but do not boil.

Tomato-French Onion Soup

1 (10 ounce) can tomato-bisque soup	280 g
2 (10 ounce) cans French onion soup	2 (280 g)
Grated parmesan cheese	
Croutons	

- In saucepan, combine soups with 2 soup cans water and heat thoroughly.

- To serve, pour soup into individual bowls and top with croutons and cheese.

Easy Potato Soup

1 (16 ounce) package frozen hash brown potatoes	.5 kg
1 cup chopped onion	240 ml
1 (14 ounce) can chicken broth	396 g
1 (10 ounce) can cream of celery	280 g
1 (10 ounce) can cream of chicken soup	280 g
2 cups milk	480 ml

- In large saucepan, combine potatoes, onion and 2 cups (480 ml) water and bring to a boil. Cover, reduce heat and simmer 30 minutes.

- Stir in broth, soups and milk and heat thoroughly. (If you like, garnish with shredded cheddar cheese or cooked, diced ham.)

Fast Fiesta Soup

1 (15 ounce) can Mexican stewed tomatoes	425 g
1 (15 ounce) can whole kernel corn	425 g
1 (15 ounce) can pinto beans with liquid	425 g
2 (14 ounce) cans chicken broth	2 (396 g)
1 (10 ounce) can fiesta nacho soup	280 g
1 (12 ounce) can chicken breast with liquid	340 g

- Combine tomatoes, corn, beans, broth and nacho soup in large soup pot, heat 10 minutes over medium heat and mix well.

- Stir in chicken with liquid until thoroughly hot.

Southwestern Soup

1½ pounds lean ground beef	.7 kg
1 large onion, chopped	
2 (15 ounce) cans pinto beans with liquid	2 (425 g)
1 (15 ounce) can ranch-style beans, drained	425 g
2 (15 ounce) cans whole kernel corn	
with liquid	2 (425 g)
2 (15 ounce) cans Mexican stewed tomatoes	2 (425 g)
2 (1 ounce) packets taco seasoning	2 (28 g)

- Brown beef and onion in large soup pot, stir until beef crumbles and drain. Add beans, corn, tomatoes and 1½ cups (360 ml) water. Boil, reduce heat and stir in taco seasoning. Simmer for 25 minutes.

Speedy Vegetable Soup

1 (1 pound) lean ground beef	.5 kg
2 (15 ounce) cans stewed tomatoes	2 (425 g)
3 (14 ounce) cans beef broth	3 (396 g)
1 (16 ounce) package frozen mixed vegetables	.5 kg
½ cup instant brown rice	120 ml

- Brown beef in skillet and stir until beef crumbles. Transfer to soup pot and add tomatoes, beef broth and vegetables. Boil, reduce heat and simmer for 20 minutes and stir occasionally. Add brown rice and cook on medium heat for 5 minutes.

Chicken-Broccoli Chowder

2 (14 ounce) cans chicken broth	2 (396 g)
1 bunch fresh green onions, finely chopped, divided	
1 (10 ounce) package frozen chopped broccoli	280 g
1½ cups dry mashed potato flakes	360 ml
2½ cups cooked, cut-up chicken breasts	600 ml
1 (8 ounce) package shredded mozzarella cheese	227 g
1 (8 ounce) carton whipping cream	227 g
1 cup milk	240 ml

- Combine broth, half green onions and broccoli in large saucepan. Boil, reduce heat, cover and simmer for 5 minutes.

- Stir in dry potato flakes and mix until they blend well. Add chicken, cheese, cream, milk, 1 cup (240 ml) water and a little salt and pepper. Heat over medium heat and stir occasionally until hot and cheese melts, about 5 minutes.

- Ladle into individual soup bowls and garnish with remaining chopped green onions.

Creamy Turkey Soup

3 (14 ounce) cans chicken broth	3 (396 g)
1 pound russet potatoes, peeled, cubed	.5 kg
3 ribs celery, sliced	
1 (15 ounce) can sliced carrots, drained	425 g
1 (10 ounce) package frozen yellow squash	280 g
2 teaspoons minced garlic	10 ml
1 teaspoon dried thyme	5 ml
1½ cups shredded turkey	360 ml
1 (10 ounce) can cream of chicken soup	280 g
1 cup milk or half-and-half cream	240 ml

- Combine chicken broth, ½ cup (120 ml) water, potatoes and celery in soup pot and boil. Add a little salt and pepper and cook on medium heat about 20 minutes or until potatoes and celery are tender. Add carrots, squash, garlic and thyme and cook another 10 minutes.

- Stir in shredded turkey, chicken soup and milk and heat just until soup is thoroughly hot, but do not boil.

Across-the-Border Tamale Soup

1 pound lean ground beef	.5 kg
1 (16 ounce) package frozen chopped onions and bell peppers	.5 kg
2 tablespoons oil	30 ml
1 (10 ounce) package frozen corn	280 g
2 (14 ounce) cans beef broth	2 (396 g)
1 (15 ounce) can pinto beans with liquid	425 g
2 tablespoons chili powder	30 ml
1 teaspoon ground cumin	5 ml
1 (28 ounce) can tamales, shucked, quartered with liquid	794 g

- In large skillet, brown beef, onions and bell peppers in oil.

- Transfer to soup pot and add corn, broth, beans, chili powder, cumin and a little salt and pepper.

- Boil, reduce heat and simmer for 30 minutes. About 15 minutes prior to serving, add tamale chunks and heat thoroughly. Stir gently so tamales will not break. Serve hot.

TIP: For a spicier soup, you could add 1 (10 ounce/280 g) can tomatoes and green chilies.

Meatball Soup

1 (18 ounce) package frozen, cooked Italian meatballs	510 g
2 (14 ounce) cans beef broth	2 (396 g)
2 (15 ounce) cans Italian stewed tomatoes	2 (425 g)
1 (16 ounce) package frozen stew vegetables	.5 kg

- Place meatballs, beef broth and tomatoes in large saucepan. Boil, reduce heat and simmer 10 minutes or until meatballs are thoroughly hot. Add vegetables and cook on medium heat for 10 minutes.

TIP: For thicker soup, mix 2 tablespoons (30 ml) cornstarch in ¼ cup (60 ml) water. Add to soup, boil and stir until soup thickens.

Potato-Sausage Soup

1 pound pork sausage link	.5 kg
1 cup chopped celery	240 ml
1 cup chopped onion	240 ml
2 (10 ounce) cans potato soup	2 (280 g)
1 (14 ounce) can chicken broth	396 g

- Cut sausage into 1-inch (2.5 cm) diagonal slices. Brown sausage in large heavy soup pot, drain and place in separate bowl. Leave about 2 tablespoons (30 ml) sausage drippings in skillet and saute celery and onion.

- Add potato soup, ¾ cup (180 ml) water, chicken broth and sausage. Boil, reduce heat and simmer for 20 minutes.

Blue Norther Stew

Cold fronts in the south are called northers.
This is a great choice for one of those cold, winter days.

1½ pounds lean ground beef	.7 kg
1 onion, chopped	
1 (1 ounce) packet taco seasoning	28 g
1 (1 ounce) packet ranch dressing mix	28 g
1 (15 ounce) can whole kernel corn, drained	425 g
1 (15 ounce) can kidney beans with liquid	425 g
2 (15 ounce) cans pinto beans	2 (425 g)
2 (15 ounce) cans Mexican stewed tomatoes	2 (425 g)
1 (10 ounce) can tomatoes and green chilies	280 g

- Brown ground beef and onion in large roasting pan. Add both packets seasonings and mix well.

- Add corn, beans, stewed tomatoes, tomatoes and green chilies and 1 cup water, mix well and simmer for about 30 minutes.

Beefy Bean Chili

2 pounds lean ground beef	1 kg
3 ribs celery, sliced	
1 onion, chopped	
1 bell pepper, seeded, chopped	
2 teaspoons minced garlic	10 ml
1 (15 ounce) can tomato sauce	425 g
3 tablespoons chili powder	45 ml
2 (15 ounce) cans pinto beans with liquid	2 (425 g)
1 - 2 cups crushed tortilla chips	240 ml

- Brown and cook ground beef in large soup pot over medium heat until meat crumbles. Add celery, onion, bell pepper and minced garlic. Cook for 5 minutes or until vegetables are tender, but not brown.

- Stir in tomato sauce, chili powder, 2 cups (480 ml) water and a little salt and pepper and mix well. Bring mixture to a boil, reduce heat and simmer for 35 minutes.

- Add beans during last 15 minutes of cooking time. Ladle into individual serving bowls and top each serving with several tablespoons crushed tortilla chips.

Hearty Bean and Ham Soup

What a great supper for a cold winter night!

¼ cup (½ stick) butter	60 ml
1 (15 ounce) can sliced carrots, drained	425 g
1 cup chopped celery	240 ml
1 cup chopped green bell pepper	240 ml
2 - 3 cups cooked, diced ham	480 ml
2 (15 ounce) cans navy beans with liquid	2 (425 g)
2 (15 ounce) cans jalapeno pinto beans with liquid	2 (425 g)
2 (14 ounce) cans chicken broth	2 (396 g)
2 teaspoons chili powder	10 ml

- Cook carrots, celery and bell pepper in soup pot with butter about 8 minutes until tender-crisp.

- Add diced ham, navy beans, pinto beans, chicken broth, chili powder and a little salt and pepper. Boil and stir constantly for 3 minutes. Reduce heat and simmer for 15 minutes.

TIP: Cornbread is great with this and it's so quick and easy to make. If you want to fix it, just buy 2 (8 ounce/227 g) packages corn muffin mix. Add 2 eggs and ⅔ cup (160 ml) milk, mix it up and pour it into sprayed 7 x 11-inch 18 x 28 cm) baking pan. Bake according to package directions.

Soup with an Attitude

1 (32 ounce) carton chicken broth	1 kg
3 baked potatoes, peeled, grated	
2 onions, finely chopped	
3 ribs celery, sliced	
1 (8 ounce) can peas, drained	227 g
1 (7 ounce) can green chilies	198 g
3 cups chopped ham	710 ml
1 (16 ounce) package cubed Mexican	
Velveeta® cheese	.5 kg
1 (1 pint) half-and-half cream	.5 kg

- Combine broth, potatoes, onions, celery, peas, chilies and ham in soup pot. While stirring, bring to a boil, reduce heat to medium-low and simmer 30 minutes.

- On medium heat, add cheese and stir constantly until cheese melts. Stir in cream and continue cooking until soup is thoroughly hot; do not boil.

Cabbage-Ham Soup

1 (16 ounce) package cabbage slaw	.5 kg
1 onion, chopped	
1 red bell pepper, seeded, chopped	
1 teaspoon minced garlic	5 ml
2 (14 ounce) cans chicken broth	2 (396 g)
1 (15 ounce) can stewed tomatoes	425 g
2 cups cooked, cubed ham	480 ml
¼ cup packed brown sugar	60 ml
2 tablespoon lemon juice	30 ml

- Combine cabbage, onion, bell pepper, garlic, chicken broth and 1 cup water in large, heavy soup pot. Boil, reduce heat and simmer for 20 minutes.

- Stir in tomatoes, ham, 1 teaspoon (5 ml) salt, brown sugar, lemon juice and a little pepper. Heat just until soup is thoroughly hot.

Clam Chowder

1 (10 ounce) can New England clam chowder	280 g
1 (10 ounce) can cream of celery soup	280 g
1 (10 ounce) can cream of potato soup	280 g
1 (6 ounce) can chopped clams	168 g
1 (10 ounce) soup can milk	280 g

- Combine all ingredients in saucepan. Heat and stir.

Ham and Corn Chowder

3 medium potatoes, cubed
2 (14 ounce) cans chicken broth, divided   2 (396 g)
2 ribs celery, chopped
1 onion, chopped
4 tablespoons flour   60 ml
1 (1 pint) half-and-half cream   .5 kg
½ teaspoon cayenne pepper   2 ml
1 (15 ounce) can whole kernel corn   425 g
1 (15 ounce) can cream-style corn   425 g
3 cups cooked, cubed ham   710 ml
1 (8 ounce) package shredded Velveeta® cheese   227 g

- Cook potatoes with 1 can chicken broth in saucepan. Saute celery and onion in large soup pot with a little oil.

- On medium heat add flour and mix well. Add second can broth and half-and-half. Cook, stirring constantly, until mixture thickens.

- Add potatoes, cayenne pepper, corn, cream-style corn, ham, cheese and a little salt and pepper. Heat slowly and stir several times to keep from sticking.

When you're pouring soup or stew from one container to another, pour it over the back of a large spoon. The spoon will reduce the splatter and the process will be neater with less clean-up.

Rich Corn Chowder

8 ears fresh corn	
8 slices bacon	
1 small onion, chopped	
½ red bell pepper, seeded, chopped	
1 small baking potato, peeled, cubed	
1 (1 pint) half-and-half cream	.5 kg
2 teaspoons sugar	10 ml
½ teaspoon dried thyme	2 ml
1 tablespoon cornstarch	15 ml

- Cut corn from cobs into large bowl and scrape well to remove all milk.

- Fry bacon in large soup pot over medium heat, remove bacon and save drippings in pan. Crumble bacon and set aside.

- Cook onion and bell pepper in drippings until tender. Stir in corn, potato, 1 cup (240 ml) water and a little salt and pepper. Boil, cover, reduce heat and simmer for 15 minutes, stirring occasionally.

- Stir in 1½ cups (360 ml) cream, sugar and thyme. Combine cornstarch and remaining cream and stir until smooth. Gradually add to corn mixture and stir constantly.

- Cook uncovered for 15 minutes, stirring constantly, until soup thickens.

Sausage-Vegetable Soup

1 pound bulk Italian sausage	.5 kg
2 onions, chopped	
2 teaspoons minced garlic	10 ml
1 (1 ounce) packet beefy soup mix	28 g
1 (15 ounce) can sliced carrots, drained	425 g
2 (15 ounce) cans Italian stewed tomatoes	2 (425 g)
2 (15 ounce) cans garbanzo beans, drained	2 (425 g)
1 cup elbow macaroni	240 ml

- Brown sausage, onions and garlic in large soup pot. Drain and add 4 cups (1 L) water, soup mix, carrots, tomatoes and garbanzo beans. Boil, reduce heat and simmer for 25 minutes.

- Add elbow macaroni and continue cooking additional 15 to 20 minutes or until macaroni is tender.

Super Easy Gumbo

1 (10 ounce) can pepper-pot soup	280 g
1 (10 ounce) can chicken gumbo soup	280 g
1 (6 ounce) can white crabmeat, flaked	168 g
1 (6 ounce) can tiny shrimp, drained	168 g

- Combine all ingredients with 1½ soup cans water in saucepan.

- Cover and simmer for 15 minutes.

Seafood Bisque

¼ cup (½ stick) butter	60 ml
1 (8 ounce) package frozen salad shrimp, thawed	227 g
1 (6 ounce) can crab, drained, flaked	168 g
1 (15 ounce) can whole new potatoes, drained, sliced	425 g
1 teaspoon minced garlic	5 ml
½ cup flour	120 ml
2 (14 ounce) cans chicken broth, divided	2 (396 g)
1 cup half-and-half cream	240 ml

- Melt butter and cook on medium heat in large saucepan. Add shrimp, crab, new potatoes and garlic and cook for 10 minutes.

- Stir in flour and cook, stirring constantly, for 3 minutes. Gradually add chicken broth, cook and stir until mixture thickens.

- Stir in cream and a little salt and pepper, stirring constantly and cook just until mixture is thoroughly hot; do not boil.

The best way to keep cleaned fish from getting freezer burn is to fill a plastic bag about half full of water. Add fish and add more water so fish is covered. Seal and record the date the fish is frozen.

Fresh Oyster Stew

2 pints fresh oysters with liquor	1 kg
3 slices bacon	
1 small onion, chopped	
2 ribs celery, chopped	
1 (4 ounce) can sliced mushrooms	114 g
1 (10 ounce) can cream of potato soup	280 g
3 cups half-and-half cream	710 ml
⅓ cup fresh chopped parsley	80 ml

- Drain oysters and save liquor. Fry bacon until crisp, drain bacon and crumble. Set aside.

- On medium heat in large skillet, cook onion and celery in bacon fat until tender.

- Add mushrooms, soup, oyster liquor, cream and a little salt and pepper. Heat over medium heat, stirring occasionally, until mixture is thoroughly hot.

- Stir in bacon and oysters and heat 4 to 5 minutes longer or until edges of oysters begin to curl. Sprinkle with parsley.

A real time-saver is to make a large pot of soup or stew and freeze it in portions in large plastic bags. Freeze enough for one, two or four. When the bag is sealed, it will lay flat in the freezer and won't take up as much room as containers. Be sure to leave a little room for expansion as it freezes.

Incredible Broccoli-Cheese Soup

This really is an incredible soup!

1 (10 ounce) package frozen chopped broccoli	280 g
3 tablespoons butter	45 ml
¼ onion, finely chopped	
¼ cup flour	60 ml
1 (1 pint) carton half-and-half cream	.5 kg
1 (14 ounce) can chicken broth	396 g
⅛ teaspoon cayenne pepper	.5 ml
1 (8 ounce) package mild Mexican, cubed, Velveeta® cheese	117 g

- Punch several holes in broccoli package and microwave for 5 minutes. Turn package in microwave and cook another 4 minutes. Leave in microwave for 3 minutes.

- Melt butter and saute onion in large saucepan, but do not brown. Add flour, stir and gradually add cream, chicken broth, ½ teaspoon (2 ml) salt, ⅛ teaspoon (.5 ml) pepper and cayenne pepper. Stir constantly and heat until mixture is slightly thick. Do not let mixture boil!

- Add cheese, stir constantly and heat until cheese melts. Add cooked broccoli. Serve piping hot.

Southwestern Bean Soup

*Don't let the number of ingredients discourage you. Ask yourself
this question, "Can I open cans?"*

¼ cup (½ stick) butter	60 ml
1 onion, chopped	
1 bell pepper, seeded, chopped	
2 teaspoons minced garlic	10 ml
2 (15 ounce) cans Mexican stewed tomatoes	2 (425 g)
1 (15 ounce) can pinto beans, drained	425 g
1 (15 ounce) can kidney beans, rinsed, drained	425 g
1 (15 ounce) can black beans, rinsed, drained	425 g
1 tablespoon chili powder	15 ml
¼ teaspoon ground coriander	1 ml
1 cup shredded Mexican 4-cheese blend	240 ml
1 cup shredded Monterey Jack, divided	240 ml

- Melt butter in large saucepan on medium heat and
  cook onion, bell pepper and garlic for 5 minutes. Stir
  in tomatoes, all 3 cans beans, chili powder, coriander
  and a little salt and pepper.

- Boil, reduce heat, cover and simmer for 25 minutes.

- Stir in Mexican cheese and cook over low heat,
  stirring occasionally, just until cheese melts.

- Ladle into individual soup bowls and sprinkle Jack
  cheese over each serving.

Italian Minestrone

1 (16 ounce) package frozen onions and bell peppers	.5 kg
3 ribs celery, chopped	
2 teaspoons minced garlic	10 ml
¼ cup (½ stick) butter	60 ml
2 (15 ounce) cans diced tomatoes	2 (425 g)
1 teaspoon dried oregano	5 ml
1 teaspoon dried basil	5 ml
2 (14 ounce) cans beef broth	2 (396 g)
2 (15 ounce) cans navy beans	2 (425 g)
2 medium zucchini, cut in half lengthwise, sliced	
1 cup elbow macaroni	240 ml

■ Saute onions, bell peppers, celery and garlic in butter for about 2 minutes in soup pot. Add tomatoes, oregano, basil and a little salt and pepper. Boil, reduce heat and simmer for 15 minutes, stirring occasionally.

■ Stir in beef broth, beans, zucchini and macaroni and boil. Reduce heat and simmer another 15 minutes or until macaroni is tender.

Broccoli-Noodle Salad

1 cup slivered almonds, toasted	240 ml
1 cup sunflower seeds, toasted	240 ml
2 (3 ounce) packages chicken-flavored ramen noodles	2 (84 g)
1 (16 ounce) package broccoli slaw	.5 kg
1 (8 ounce) bottle Italian salad dressing	227 g

- Toast almonds and sunflower seeds in oven at 275Y (135° C) for about 10 minutes.

- Break up ramen noodles and mix with slaw, almonds and sunflower seeds. Toss with Italian salad dressing and chill.

Winter Salad

1 (15 ounce) can cut green beans, drained	425 g
1 (15 ounce) can English peas, drained	425 g
1 (15 ounce) can whole kernel corn, drained	425 g
1 (15 ounce) can jalapeno black-eyed peas, drained	425 g
1 (8 ounce) bottle Italian salad dressing	227 g

- Combine all vegetables in large bowl. (Add chopped onion and chopped bell pepper if you have it handy.)

- Pour Italian dressing over vegetables. Cover and refrigerate.

Nutty Green Salad

6 cups torn, mixed salad greens	1.5 L
1 medium zucchini, sliced	
1 (8 ounce) can sliced water chestnuts, drained	227 g
½ cup peanuts	120 ml
⅓ cup Italian salad dressing	80 ml

- Toss greens, zucchini, water chestnuts and peanuts.
- When ready to serve, add salad dressing and toss.

Green and Red Salad

4 cups torn mixed salad green	1 L
3 fresh green onions with tops, chopped	
2 medium red apples, diced	
1 cup fresh raspberries	240 ml
½ cup poppy seed dressing	120 ml

- In bowl, toss salad greens, onions and fruit.
- Drizzle with dressing and toss.

Special Rice Salad

1 (6 ounce) package chicken-flavored rice and macaroni	168 g
¾ cup chopped green pepper	180 ml
1 bunch fresh green onion with tops, chopped	
2 (6 ounce) jars marinated artichoke hearts	2 (168 g)
½ - ⅔ cup mayonnaise	120 ml

- Cook rice and macaroni according to directions (but with no butter), drain and cool.

- Add green pepper, onions, artichoke hearts and mayonnaise, toss and chill.

Chicken Salad

3 cups boneless, skinless chicken breast halves, cooked, chopped	710 ml
1½ cups chopped celery	360 ml
½ cup sweet pickle relish	120 ml
2 eggs, hard-boiled, chopped	
¾ cup mayonnaise	180 ml

- Combine all ingredients and several sprinkles salt and pepper.

Fantastic Fruit Salad

2 (11 ounce) cans mandarin oranges	2 (312 g)
2 (15 ounce) cans pineapple chunks	2 (425 g)
1 (16 ounce) carton frozen strawberries, thawed	.5 kg
1 (20 ounce) can peach pie filling	567 g
1 (20 ounce) can apricot pie filling	567 g

- Drain oranges, pineapple and strawberries.

- Combine all ingredients and fold together gently.

TIP: If you have several bananas, add them too.

Peachy Fruit Salad

2 (20 ounce) cans peach pie filling	2 (567 g)
1 (20 ounce) can pineapple chunks, drained	567 g
1 (11 ounce) can mandarin oranges, drained	312 g
1 (8 ounce) jar maraschino cherries, drained	227 g
1 cup miniature marshmallows	240 ml

- Combine all ingredients in large bowl, fold together gently and refrigerate.

- Serve in pretty crystal bowl. (Bananas may be added if you like.)

Cherry Salad

1 (20 ounce) can cherry pie filling	567 g
1 (20 ounce) can crushed pineapple, drained	567 g
1 (14 ounce) can sweetened condensed milk	396 g
1 cup miniature marshmallows	240 ml
1 cup chopped pecans	240 ml
1 (8 ounce) carton whipped topping	227 g

- In large bowl, combine pie filling, pineapple, sweetened condensed milk, marshmallows and pecans.

- Fold in whipped topping, chill and serve in pretty crystal bowl. Add a couple drops of red food coloring for a brighter color.

Butter-Mint Salad

1 (6 ounce) box lime gelatin	168 g
1 (20 ounce) can crushed pineapple with juice	567 g
½ (10 ounce) bag miniature marshmallows	½ (280 g)
1 (8 ounce) carton whipped topping	227 g
1 (8 ounce) bag butter mints, crushed	227 g

- Pour dry gelatin over pineapple. Add marshmallows and set overnight.

- Fold in whipped topping and butter mints. Pour into 9 x 13-inch (23 x 33 cm) dish and freeze.

Divinity Salad

1 (6 ounce) package lemon gelatin	168 g
1 (8 ounce) package cream cheese, softened	227 g
¾ cup chopped pecans	180 ml
1 (15 ounce) can crushed pineapple with juice	425 g
1 (8 ounce) carton whipped topping	227 g

- With mixer, blend gelatin with 1 cup boiling water until it dissolves.

- Add cream cheese, beat slowly and increase speed until smooth. Add pecans and pineapple and cool in refrigerator until nearly set. Fold in whipped topping. Pour into 9 x 13-inch (23 x 33 cm) dish and refrigerate.

Cherry Cranberry Salad

1 (6 ounce) package cherry gelatin	168 g
1 (20 ounce) can cherry pie filling	567 g
1 (16 ounce) can whole cranberry sauce	.5 kg

- In mixing bowl, combine cherry gelatin and 1 cup boiling water and mix until gelatin dissolves.

- Mix pie filling and cranberry sauce into gelatin.

- Pour into 9 x 13-inch (23 x 33 cm) dish and refrigerate.

Deviled Eggs

6 eggs, hard-boiled
2 tablespoons sweet pickle relish   30 ml
3 tablespoons mayonnaise   45 ml
½ teaspoon mustard   2 ml

- Peel eggs and cut in half lengthwise.

- Remove yolks and mash with fork.

- Add relish, mayonnaise and mustard to yolks and place yolk mixture back into egg white halves.

- Sprinkle with paprika, if you like.

Sunshine Salad

2 (15 ounce) cans Mexicorn®, drained   2 (425 g)
2 (15 ounce) cans peas, drained   2 (425 g)
1 (15 ounce) can kidney beans, rinsed, drained   425 g
1 (8 ounce) bottle Italian salad dressing   227 g

- In large bowl, combine corn, peas and beans.

- Pour dressing over vegetables and chill for several hours before serving.

Swiss Salad

1 large head romaine lettuce
1 bunch fresh green onions with tops, chopped
1 (8 ounce) package shredded Swiss cheese   227 g
½ cup toasted sunflower seeds   120 ml

- Tear lettuce into bite-size pieces. Add onions, cheese and sunflower seeds and toss.

- Serve with vinaigrette salad dressing.

Vinaigrette for Swiss Salad:
⅔ cup salad oil   160 ml
⅓ cup red wine vinegar   80 ml
1 tablespoon seasoned salt   15 ml

- Combine all ingredients and chill.

Carrot Salad

3 cups finely grated carrots   710 ml
1 (8 ounce) can crushed pineapple, drained   227 g
4 tablespoons flaked coconut   60 ml
1 tablespoon sugar   15 ml
⅓ cup mayonnaise   80 ml

- Combine carrots, pineapple, coconut and sugar and mix well. Toss with mayonnaise and chill.

Stuffed Cucumber Slices

3 cucumbers, peeled
2 (3 ounce) packages cream cheese, softened   2 (84 g)
¼ cup stuffed green olives, chopped   60 ml
½ teaspoon seasoned salt   2 ml

- Halve cucumbers lengthwise and scoop out seeds.

- Beat cream cheese with mixer until creamy and add olives and seasoned salt. Fill hollows of cucumbers with cream cheese mixture.

- Press halves back together, wrap tightly in plastic wrap and chill.

- Remove plastic wrap and cut crosswise in ⅓-inch (.8 cm) slices to serve.

Broccoli-Waldorf Salad

6 cups fresh broccoli florets   1.5 L
1 large red apple with peel, chopped
½ cup golden raisins   120 ml
½ cup chopped pecans   120 ml
½ cup prepared coleslaw dressing   120 ml

- In large bowl, combine broccoli, apple, raisins and pecans. Drizzle with dressing, toss to coat and refrigerate. Serve in pretty crystal bowl.

Color-Coded Salad

1 (16 ounce) package tri-colored macaroni, cooked, drained	.5 kg
1 red bell pepper, cut into julienne strips	
1 cup chopped zucchini	240 ml
1 cup broccoli florets	240 ml
Caesar salad dressing	

- Combine all ingredients. Toss with 1 cup (240 ml) salad dressing and chill.

Nutty Cranberry Relish

1 pound fresh cranberries	.5 kg
2¼ cups sugar	540 ml
1 cup chopped pecans, toasted	240 ml
1 cup orange marmalade	240 ml

- Preheat oven to 350° (176° C).

- Wash and drain cranberries and mix with sugar.

- Place in 1-quart (1 L) baking dish, cover and bake for   1 hour.

- Add marmalade and pecans to cranberry mixture. Mix well, pour into container and chill before serving.

Pistachio Salad or Dessert

1 (20 ounce) can crushed pineapple with juice	567 g
1 (3 ounce) package instant pistachio pudding	84 g
2 cups miniature marshmallows	480 ml
1 cup chopped pecans	240 ml
1 (8 ounce) carton whipped topping	227 g

- Place pineapple in large bowl and sprinkle with dry pudding mix.
- Add marshmallows and pecans and fold in whipped topping. Pour into crystal serving dish and chill.

Broccoli-Chicken Salad

3 - 4 boneless, skinless chicken breast halves, cooked, cubed	
2 cups fresh broccoli florets	480 ml
1 sweet red bell pepper, seeded, chopped	
1 cup chopped celery	240 ml
Honey-mustard salad dressing	

- Combine all ingredients.
- Toss mixture with honey-mustard salad dressing and chill.

Cottage Cheese-Fruit Salad

1 (6 ounce) package orange gelatin	168 g
1 (16 ounce) carton small curd cottage cheese	.5 kg
2 (11 ounce) cans mandarin oranges, drained	2 (312 g)
1 (20 ounce) can chunk pineapple, drained	567 g
1 (8 ounce) carton whipped topping	227 g

- Sprinkle gelatin over cottage cheese and mix well.

- Add oranges and pineapple and mix well. Fold in whipped topping, chill and serve in pretty crystal bowl.

Pink Salad

1 (6 ounce) package raspberry gelatin	168 g
1 (20 ounce) can crushed pineapple with juice	567 g
1 cup cream-style cottage cheese	240 ml
1 (8 ounce) carton whipped topping	227 g
¼ cup chopped pecans	60 ml

- Place gelatin in large bowl.

- Combine juice from pineapple and, if necessary, enough water to make 1¼ cups (300 ml) liquid. Heat, pour over gelatin and mix well.

- Cool in refrigerator just until gelatin begins to thicken. Fold in cottage cheese, whipped topping and pecans.

- Pour into molds or 9 x 13-inch (23 x 33 cm) dish and refrigerate.

Cranapple Wiggle

A family friend made this recipe a tradition.

1 (6 ounce) package cherry gelatin	168 g
1 (16 ounce) can whole cranberry sauce	.5 kg
1 (15 ounce) can crushed pineapple with juice	425 g
1 cup chopped apples	240 ml
1 cup chopped pecans	240 ml

- Dissolve gelatin in 1½ cups (360 ml) boiling water and mix well.

- Add cranberry sauce, pineapple, apples and pecans.

- Pour into sprayed 9 x 13-inch (23 x 33 cm) glass dish and chill. Stir about the time it begins to set so the apples will not all stay on top. Serves 12.

Apple-Pineapple Salad

1 (6 ounce) package lemon gelatin	168 g
1 (15 ounce) can pineapple tidbits with juice	425 g
1 cup diced apples with peel	240 ml
1 cup chopped pecans	240 ml

- Dissolve gelatin in 1 cup (240 ml) boiling water.

- Add pineapple and place in refrigerator until slightly thick. Fold in apples and pecans.

- Pour into solid mold or 7 x 11-inch (18 x 28 cm) dish and chill until firm.

Frozen Holiday Salad

2 (3 ounce) packages cream cheese, softened   2 (84 g)
3 tablespoons mayonnaise   45 ml
¼ cup sugar   60 ml
1 (16 ounce) can whole cranberry sauce   .5 kg
1 (8 ounce) can crushed pineapple, drained   227 g
1 cup chopped pecans   240 ml
1 cup tiny marshmallows   240 ml
1 (8 ounce) carton whipped topping   227 g

■ Cream cheese, mayonnaise and sugar.

■ Add fruit, pecans and marshmallows and fold in
  whipped topping.

■ Pour into sprayed 9 x 13-inch (23 x 33 cm) shallow
  glass dish and freeze.

■ When ready to serve, take salad out of freezer a few
  minutes before cutting into squares.

Frozen Dessert Salad

1 (8 ounce) package cream cheese, softened	227 g
1 cup powdered sugar	240 ml
1 (10 ounce) box frozen strawberries, thawed	280 g
1 (15 ounce) can crushed pineapple, drained	425 g
1 (8 ounce) carton whipped topping	227 g

- In mixing bowl, beat cream cheese and sugar and fold in strawberries, pineapple and whipped topping. (This will be even better if you stir in ¾ cup/180 ml chopped pecans.)
- Pour into 9 x 9-inch (23 x 23 cm) pan and freeze.
- Cut into squares to serve.

If stored in an airtight container, pecans will stay fresh for 6 months in the pantry or up to a year in the freezer!

Veggie Salad

Crunchy and good!

5 zucchini, sliced paper thin
4 yellow squash, sliced paper thin
1 head cauliflower cut in bite-size pieces
1 red bell pepper, chopped
1 bunch green onions with tops, sliced
2 (2 ounce) packages slivered almonds,
   toasted   2 (57 g)
1 (8 ounce) bottle creamy Italian dressing   227 g

- Mix zucchini, yellow squash, cauliflower, bell pepper, onions, almonds, ½ teaspoon (2 ml) salt and ¼ teaspoon (1 ml) pepper.

- Add dressing and toss. Chill several hours before serving.

SIDE DISHES

Cheddar Potatoes

1 (10 ounce) can cheddar cheese soup	280 g
⅓ cup sour cream	80 ml
2 fresh green onions with tops, chopped	
3 cups instant seasoned mashed potatoes, prepared	710 ml

- Preheat oven to 350° (176° C).

- In saucepan, heat soup and add sour cream, onion and little black pepper. Stir in potatoes until they blend well.

- Pour into sprayed 2-quart (2 L) baking dish and cook for 25 minutes.

Mashed Potatoes Supreme

1 (8 ounce) package cream cheese, softened	227 g
½ cup sour cream	120 ml
2 tablespoons butter, softened	30 ml
1 (1 ounce) packet dry ranch-style salad dressing	28 g
6 - 8 cups warm instant mashed potatoes	1.5 L

- Preheat oven to 350° (176° C).

- With mixer, combine cream cheese, sour cream, butter and dressing mix and mix well. Add potatoes and stir well.

- Transfer to 2-quart (2 L) baking dish and bake for 25 minutes or until hot throughout.

Potatoes Supreme

1 (32 ounce) package frozen hash browned potatoes, thawed	1 kg
1 onion, chopped	
2 (10 ounce) cans cream of chicken soup	2 (280 g)
1 (8 ounce) carton sour cream	227 g

- Preheat oven to 350° (176° C).

- In large bowl, combine all ingredients and mix well.

- Pour into sprayed 9 x 13-inch (23 x 33 cm) baking dish. Bake covered for 1 hour.

Tip: Sprinkle ½ cup (120 ml) parmesan or cheddar cheese on top before the last 5 minutes of baking.

Potatoes au Gratin

1 (8 ounce) package cubed Velveeta® cheese	227 g
1 (16 ounce) carton half-and-half cream	.5 kg
1 cup shredded cheddar cheese	240 ml
½ cup (1 stick) butter	120 ml
1 (32 ounce) package frozen hash brown potatoes, thawed	1 kg

- Preheat oven to 350° (176° C). In double boiler, melt processed cheese, half-and-half, cheese and butter. Place hash browns in sprayed 9 x 13-inch (23 x 33 cm) baking dish and pour cheese mixture over potatoes. Bake uncovered for 1 hour.

Oven Fries

5 medium baking potatoes
⅓ cup oil   80 ml
¾ teaspoon seasoned salt   4 ml
Paprika

- Preheat oven to 375° (190° C). Scrub potatoes, cut each in 6 lengthwise wedges and place in shallow baking dish.

- Combine oil, ¼ teaspoon (1 ml) pepper and seasoned salt and brush potatoes with mixture. Sprinkle potatoes lightly with paprika.

- Bake for about 50 minutes or until potatoes are tender and light brown. Baste twice with remaining oil mixture while baking.

Sweet Potatoes and Pecans

2 (17 ounce) cans sweet potatoes, drained,
  divided   2 (484 g)
1½ cups packed brown sugar   360 ml
¼ cup (½ stick) butter, melted   60 ml
1 cup chopped pecans   240 ml

- Preheat oven to 350° (176° C). Slice half sweet potatoes and place in sprayed 2-quart (2 L) baking dish.

- Combine brown sugar, butter and pecans and sprinkle half mixture over sweet potatoes. Repeat layers and bake uncovered for 30 minutes.

Scalloped Potatoes

6 medium potatoes
½ cup (1 stick) butter — 120 ml
1 tablespoon flour — 15 ml
2 cups shredded cheddar cheese — 480 ml
¾ cup milk — 180 ml

- Preheat oven to 350° (176° C).

- Peel and slice potatoes.

- Place half potatoes in sprayed 3-quart (3 L) baking dish. Slice half butter over potatoes, sprinkle with half flour and cover with half cheese.

- Repeat layers with cheese on top. Pour milk over casserole and sprinkle with a little pepper. (Prepare potatoes as fast as you can so they will not turn dark.)

- Cover and bake for 1 hour.

Twice-Baked Potatoes

8 medium baking potatoes	
2 tablespoons butter	30 ml
1 (10 ounce) can cheddar cheese soup	280 g
1 tablespoon chopped dried chives	15 ml

- Bake potatoes at 350º (176° C) for 1 hour or until done.

- Cut potatoes in half lengthwise and scoop meat from potatoes and leave thin shell.

- With mixer, whip potato meat with butter and ½ teaspoon (2 ml) salt.

- Gradually add soup and chives and beat until light and fluffy.

- Spoon mixture into potato skin shells and sprinkle with paprika.

- Bake at 425° (220° C) for 15 minutes.

TIP: If you want a little "zip" to these potatoes, add 1 (10 ounce/280 g) can fiesta nacho cheese soup instead of cheddar cheese soup.

Pasta with Basil

2½ cups small tube pasta	600 ml
1 small onion, chopped	
2 tablespoons oil	30 ml
2½ tablespoons dried basil	35 ml
1 cup shredded mozzarella cheese	240 ml

- Cook pasta according to package directions.

- In skillet, saute onion in oil.

- Stir in basil, 1 teaspoon (5 ml) salt and ¼ teaspoon (1 ml) pepper, cook and stir 1 minute.

- Drain pasta and add to basil mixture. (Leave about ½ cup water so pasta won't be too dry.)

- Remove from heat and stir in cheese just until it begins to melt.

- Serve immediately.

Creamy Fettuccine

1 (8 ounce) package fettuccine	227 g
1 pound Italian sausage	.5 kg
1 (10 ounce) can cream of mushroom soup	280 g
1 (16 ounce) carton sour cream	.5 kg

- Preheat oven to 325° (162° C).

- Cook fettuccine according to package directions and drain.

- Cut sausage into 1-inch (2.5 cm) pieces, brown over medium heat, cook for 8 minutes and drain.

- Combine all ingredients and pour into sprayed 2-quart (2 L) baking dish.

Macaroni and Cheese

1 cup macaroni	240 ml
1½ cups small curd cottage cheese	360 ml
1½ cup shredded cheddar or American cheese	360 ml
4 tablespoons grated parmesan cheese	60 ml

- Preheat oven to 350° (176° C).

- Cook macaroni according to package directions and drain. Combine all cheeses and add macaroni to cheese mixture. Spoon into sprayed 2-quart (2 L) baking dish.

- Bake covered for 35 minutes. Bake for 30 minutes.

Green Chile-Rice

1 cup cooked instant rice	240 ml
1 (12 ounce) package shredded Monterey Jack cheese	340 g
1 (7 ounce) can chopped green chilies	198 g
2 (8 ounce) cartons sour cream	2 (227 g)
½ teaspoon garlic powder	2 ml

- Preheat oven to 350° (176° C).

- In large bowl, combine and mix all ingredients and add a little salt, if you like.

- Spoon into sprayed 9 x 13-inch (23 x 33 cm) baking dish and bake for 30 minutes.

Baked Rice

2 cups rice	480 ml
½ cup (1 stick) butter, melted	120 ml
1 (10 ounce) can cream of celery soup	280 g
1 (10 ounce) can cream of onion soup	280 g

- Preheat oven to 350° (176° C).

- Combine all ingredients plus 1½ cups (360 ml) water and mix well.

- Pour into sprayed 3-quart (3 L) baking dish and bake covered for 1 hour.

Roasted Vegetables

1½ pounds assorted fresh vegetables	.7 kg
1 (11 ounce) can water chestnuts, drained	312 g
1 (1 ounce) dry savory herb with garlic soup mix	28 g
2 tablespoons butter, melted	30 ml

- Preheat oven to 400° (204° C).

- Cut all vegetables in uniform 2-inch (5 cm) pieces and place in sprayed 2-quart (2 L) baking dish with water chestnuts.

- Combine melted butter and soup mix, drizzle mixture over vegetables and stir well.

- Cover bake vegetables for 20 to 25 minutes or until tender and stir once.

- Use your favorite vegetables such as squash, carrots, red bell peppers, zucchini, cauliflower or broccoli.

Buttered Vegetables

½ cup (1 stick) butter	120 ml
2 yellow squash, sliced	
1 (16 ounce) package broccoli florets	.5 kg
1 (10 ounce) box frozen corn	280 g

- Melt butter in large skillet and combine all vegetables.

- Saute vegetables for 10 to 15 minutes or until tender-crisp. Add a little salt if you like and serve warm.

Shoe-Peg Corn Casserole

½ cup (1 stick) butter	120 ml
1 (8 ounce) package cream cheese	227 g
3 (16 ounce) cans shoe-peg corn, drained	3 (.5 kg)
1 (4 ounce) can chopped green chilies	114 g
1½ cups cracker crumbs	360 ml

- Preheat oven to 350° (176° C).

- Melt butter in saucepan, stir in cream cheese and mix until cream cheese melts.

- Add corn and chilies (and some salt and pepper, if you like), mix and pour into sprayed baking dish.

- Sprinkle cracker crumbs over casserole and bake for 25 minutes.

Fantastic Fried Corn

2 (16 ounce) packages frozen whole kernel corn	2 (.5 kg)
½ cup (1 stick) butter	120 ml
1 cup whipping cream	240 ml
1 tablespoon sugar	15 ml

- Place corn in large skillet over medium heat and add butter, whipping cream, sugar and 1 teaspoon (5 ml) salt.

- Stir constantly and heat until most of whipping cream and butter absorbs into corn.

Tasty Black-Eyed Peas

2 (10 ounce) packages frozen black-eyed peas	2 (280 g)
1¼ cups chopped green pepper	300 ml
¾ cup chopped onion	180 ml
3 tablespoons butter	45 ml
1 (15 ounce) can stewed tomatoes with liquid	425 g

- Cook black-eyed peas according to package directions and drain.

- Saute green pepper and onion in butter. Add peas, tomatoes and a little salt and pepper. Cook over low heat until thoroughly hot and stir often.

Creamed Green Peas

1 (16 ounce) package frozen English peas	.5 kg
2 tablespoons butter	30 ml
1 (10 ounce) can cream of celery soup	280 g
1 (3 ounce) package cream cheese	84 g
1 (8 ounce) can water chestnuts, drained	227 g

- Cook peas in microwave for 8 minutes and turn dish after 4 minutes.

- In large saucepan, combine butter, soup and cream cheese, cook on medium heat and stir until butter and cream cheese melt.

- Add peas and water chestnuts and mix. Serve hot.

Baked Onions

4 large onions, thinly sliced
1½ cups crushed potato chips   360 ml
1 cup shredded cheddar cheese   240 ml
1 (10 ounce) can cream of chicken soup   280 g

- Preheat oven to 300° (148° C).

- In 9 x 13-inch (23 x 33 cm) baking dish, alternate layers of onion, potato chips and cheese.

- Spoon soup over last layer and pour ¼ cup (60 ml) milk or water over top.

- Sprinkle with a little red or black pepper and bake for 1 hour.

Creamy Cabbage Bake

1 head cabbage, shredded
1 (10 ounce) can cream of celery soup   280 g
⅔ cup milk   160 ml
1 (8 ounce) package shredded cheddar cheese   227 g

- Preheat oven to 325° (162° C).

- Place cabbage in sprayed 2-quart (2 L) baking dish.

- Dilute celery soup with milk and pour over cabbage.

- Bake covered for 30 minutes.

- Remove from oven, sprinkle with cheese and bake uncovered additional 5 minutes.

Brown Sugar Carrots

2 (15 ounce) cans carrots	2 (425 g)
¼ cup (½ stick) butter	60 ml
3 tablespoons brown sugar	45 ml
1 teaspoon ground ginger	5 ml

- Drain carrots and reserve 2 tablespoons (30 ml) liquid.
- Combine reserved liquid with butter, brown sugar and ginger and heat thoroughly.
- Add carrots, stir gently and cook for 3 minutes.
- Serve hot.

Pine Nut Green Beans

1 (16 ounce) package frozen green beans	.5 kg
¼ cup (½ stick) butter	60 ml
¾ cup pine nuts	180 ml
¼ teaspoon garlic powder	1 ml

- Cook beans in water in covered 3-quart (3 L) saucepan for 10 to 15 minutes or until tender-crisp and drain.
- Melt butter in skillet over medium heat, add pine nuts and cook, stirring frequently, until golden.
- Add pine nuts to green beans and sprinkle with a little salt and pepper. Serve hot.

Parmesan Broccoli

1 (16 ounce) package frozen broccoli spears	.5 kg
½ teaspoon garlic powder	2 ml
½ cup breadcrumbs	120 ml
¼ cup (½ stick) butter, melted	60 ml
½ cup parmesan cheese	120 ml

- Cook broccoli as directed on package and drain.

- Add garlic powder, breadcrumbs, butter and cheese (and some salt, if you like) and toss.

- Heat and serve.

Crunchy Broccoli

2 (10 ounce) packages frozen broccoli florets	2 (280 g)
1 (8 ounce) can sliced water chestnuts, drained, chopped	227 g
½ cup (1 stick) butter, melted	120 ml
1 (1 ounce) packet dry onion soup mix	28 g

- Place broccoli in microwave-safe dish, cover and microwave for 5 minutes.

- Turn dish and cook another 4 minutes.

- Add water chestnuts.

- Combine melted butter and soup mix, blend well and toss with broccoli.

Broccoli-Stuffed Tomatoes

4 medium tomatoes
1 (10 ounce) package frozen chopped broccoli   280 g
1 (6 ounce) roll garlic cheese, softened   168 g
½ teaspoon garlic salt   2 ml

- Preheat oven to 375° (190° C).

- Cut tops off tomatoes and scoop out pulp.

- Cook broccoli according to package directions and drain well. Combine broccoli, cheese and garlic salt and heat just until cheese melts.

- Stuff broccoli mixture into tomatoes and place on baking sheet. Bake for about 10 minutes.

Baked Tomatoes

2 (14 ounce) cans diced tomatoes, drained   2 (396 g)
1½ cups breadcrumbs, toasted, divided   360 ml
Scant ¼ cup sugar   60 ml
½ onion, chopped
¼ cup (½ stick) butter, melted   60 ml

- Preheat oven to 325° (162° C).

- Combine tomatoes, 1 cup (240 ml) breadcrumbs, sugar, onion and butter. Pour into sprayed baking dish and cover with remaining ½ cup (120 ml) breadcrumbs. Bake for 25 to 30 minutes or until crumbs are light brown.

Baked Eggplant

1 medium eggplant	
¼ cup (½ stick) butter, melted	60 ml
1 (5 ounce) can evaporated milk	143 g
1½ cups cracker crumbs	360 ml

- Preheat oven to 350° (176° C).

- Peel, slice and boil eggplant until easily mashed and drain.

- Season with a little salt and pepper and add butter, evaporated milk and crumbs.

- Pour into sprayed 2-quart (2 L) baking dish and bake for 25 minutes.

Fried Zucchini

3 large zucchini, grated	
5 eggs	
1 tube round, buttery crackers, crushed	340 g
½ cup grated parmesan cheese	120 ml

- Combine zucchini, eggs and cracker crumbs and mix well. Add cheese and a little salt and pepper.

- Drop by spoonfuls into skillet with a little oil.

- Fry for 15 minutes and brown on each side.

TIP: One tube round buttery crackers is one-third of 1 (12 ounce/340 g) box.

Baked Squash

5 cups cooked squash, drained	1.3 L
¾ cup shredded Monterey Jack cheese	180 ml
1 (10 ounce) can cream of chicken soup	280 g
1 (6 ounce) box herb dressing mix	168 g

- Preheat oven to 375° (190° C).

- Place cooked squash in mixing bowl and season with a little salt. Add cheese and soup and blend well.

- Mix dressing according to package directions and place half dressing in sprayed 9 x 13-inch (23 x 33 cm) baking dish.

- Spoon in squash mixture and sprinkle remaining dressing on top.

- Bake uncovered for 30 minutes.

Chile-Cheese Squash

1 pound yellow squash	.5 kg
⅔ cup mayonnaise	160 ml
1 (4 ounce) can diced green chilies, drained	114 g
⅔ cup shredded longhorn cheese	160 ml
⅔ cup breadcrumbs	160 ml

- Cook squash in salted water just until tender-crisp and drain.

- Return squash to saucepan and stir in mayonnaise, chilies, cheese and breadcrumbs. Serve hot.

Stuffed Yellow Squash

5 large yellow squash
1 (16 ounce) package frozen chopped spinach .5 kg
1 (8 ounce) package cream cheese, cubed 227 g
1 (1 ounce) packet dry onion soup mix 28 g
Shredded cheddar cheese

■ Preheat oven to 325° (162° C). Steam squash whole until tender. Slit squash lengthwise and remove seeds with spoon.

■ Cook spinach according to package directions and drain well. Add cream cheese to cooked spinach and stir until it melts. (Do not let boil.)

■ Add soup mix and blend well. Fill scooped out squash shells with spinach mixture and top with few sprinkles cheese. Place on baking sheet and bake for 15 minutes.

Zucchini Bake

4 cups grated zucchini 1 L
1½ cups shredded Monterey Jack cheese 360 ml
4 eggs, beaten
2 cups cheese cracker crumbs 480 ml

■ Preheat oven to 350° (176° C).

■ In bowl, combine zucchini, cheese and eggs and mix well. Spoon into sprayed 3-quart (3 L) baking dish and sprinkle cracker crumbs over top.

■ Bake uncovered for 35 minutes.

Creamed-Spinach Bake

2 (10 ounce) packages frozen chopped spinach	2 (280 g)
2 (3 ounce) packages cream cheese, softened	2 (84 g)
3 tablespoons butter	45 ml
1 cup seasoned breadcrumbs	240 ml

- Preheat oven to 350° (176° C).

- Cook spinach according to package directions and drain.

- Combine cream cheese and butter with spinach and heat until they melt and mix well with spinach.

- Pour into sprayed 2-quart (2L) baking dish and sprinkle a little salt over spinach.

- Cover with breadcrumbs and bake for 15 to 20 minutes.

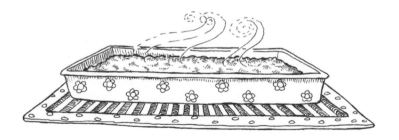

Spinach Casserole

1 (16 ounce) package frozen chopped spinach	.5 kg
1 (8 ounce) package cream cheese and chives	227 g
1 (10 ounce) can cream of mushroom soup	280 g
1 egg, beaten	
Cracker crumbs	

- Preheat oven to 350° (176° C).

- Cook spinach according to package directions and drain.

- Blend cream cheese and soup with egg, mix with spinach and pour into 2-quart (2L) sprayed baking dish.

- Top with cracker crumbs and bake for 35 minutes.

Savory Cauliflower

1 head cauliflower	
1 (1 ounce) package hollandaise sauce mix	28 g
Fresh parsley	
Lemon slices, optional	

- Cut cauliflower into small florets and cook in salted water until barely tender. (Be VERY careful not to overcook cauliflower.)

- Mix sauce according to package directions.

- Drain cauliflower, top with sauce and sprinkle with parsley. Garnish with lemon slices, if you like.

Cauliflower Medley

1 head cauliflower, cut into florets
1 (14 ounce) can Italian stewed tomatoes
   with juice 396 g
1 bell pepper, chopped
1 onion, chopped
¼ cup (½ stick) butter 60 ml
1 cup shredded cheddar cheese 240 ml

- Preheat oven to 350° (176° C).

- Place cauliflower, stewed tomatoes, bell pepper, onion and butter in large saucepan with about 2 tablespoons (30 ml) water and some salt and pepper.

- Cook in saucepan with lid until cauliflower is done, about 10 to 15 minutes. (Do not let cauliflower get mushy.)

- Place in 2-quart (2 L) baking dish and sprinkle cheese on top.

- Bake just until cheese melts.

Asparagus Bake

4 (10 ounce) cans asparagus	4 (280 g)
3 eggs, hard-boiled, sliced	
⅓ cup milk	80 ml
1½ cups shredded cheddar cheese	360 ml
1¼ cups cheese cracker crumbs	300 ml

- Preheat oven to 350° (176° C).

- Place asparagus in 7 x 11-inch (18 x 28 cm) baking dish, layer hard-boiled eggs on top and pour milk over casserole.

- Sprinkle cheese on top and add cracker crumbs.

- Bake, uncovered for 30 minutes.

Sesame Asparagus

6 fresh asparagus spears, trimmed	
1 tablespoon butter	15 ml
1 teaspoon lemon juice	5 ml
1 teaspoon sesame seeds	5 ml

- Place asparagus in skillet (sprinkle with salt if desired), add ¼ cup (60 ml) water and bring to a boil.

- Reduce heat, cover and simmer for 4 minutes.

- Melt butter and add lemon juice and sesame seeds.

- Drain asparagus and drizzle with butter mixture.

Baked Beans

2 (15 ounce) cans pork and beans,	
slightly drained	2 (425 g)
½ onion, finely chopped	
⅔ cup packed brown sugar	160 ml
¼ cup chili sauce	60 ml
1 tablespoon Worcestershire sauce	15 ml
2 strips bacon	

- Preheat oven to 325° (162° C).

- In bowl, combine beans, onion, brown sugar, chili sauce and Worcestershire. Pour into sprayed 2-quart (2 L) baking dish and place bacon strips over bean mixture.

- Bake uncovered for 50 minutes.

Creamy Vegetable Casserole

1 (16 ounce) package frozen broccoli, carrots and cauliflower	.5 kg
1 (10 ounce) can cream of mushroom soup	280 g
1 (8 ounce) carton garden vegetable cream cheese	227 g
1 cup seasoned croutons	240 ml

- Preheat oven to 375° (190° C).

- Cook vegetables according to package directions, drain and place in large bowl.

- Place soup and cream cheese in saucepan and heat just enough to mix easily.

- Pour soup mixture into vegetable mixture, stir well and pour into 2-quart (2 L) baking dish.

- Sprinkle with croutons and bake uncovered for 25 minutes or until bubbly.

Corn Vegetable Medley

1 (10 ounce) can golden corn soup	280 g
½ cup milk	120 ml
2 cups fresh broccoli florets	480 ml
2 cups cauliflower florets	480 ml
1 cup shredded cheddar cheese	240 ml

- In saucepan over medium heat, heat soup and milk to boiling and stir often.

- Stir in broccoli and cauliflower florets and return to boiling.

- Reduce heat to low and cover. Cook 20 minutes or until vegetables are tender and stir occasionally.

- Stir in cheese and heat until cheese melts.

Calico Corn

1 (16 ounce) package frozen whole kernel corn	.5 kg
1 bell pepper, chopped	
⅓ cup chopped celery	80 ml
1 (10 ounce) can cheddar cheese soup	280 g

- Preheat oven to 350° (176° C).

- Cook corn in microwave according to package directions and drain well. Add bell pepper and celery. Stir in soup and mix well.

- Pour into sprayed 2-quart (2 L) baking dish and bake covered for 30 minutes.

Cheesy Beefy Gnocchi

1 pound lean ground beef	.5 kg
1 (10 ounce) can cheddar cheese soup	280 g
1 (10 ounce) can tomato-bisque soup	280 g
2 cups gnocchi or shell pasta	480 ml

- In skillet, cook beef until brown and drain.
- Add soups, pasta and 1½ cups (360 ml) water and bring mixture to a boil.
- Cover and cook over medium heat for 10 to 12 minutes or until pasta is done. Stir often.

Chili Casserole

1 (40 ounce) can chili with beans	1.1 kg
2 (4 ounce) cans chopped green chilies	2 (114 g)
1 (2 ounce) can sliced ripe olives, drained	57 g
1 (8 ounce) package shredded cheddar cheese	227 g
2 cups crushed ranch-flavored tortilla chips	480 ml

- Preheat oven to 350° (176° C).
- Combine all ingredients and transfer to sprayed 3-quart (3 L) baking dish.
- Bake uncovered for 35 minutes or until bubbly.

Potato-Beef Casserole

4 medium potatoes, peeled, sliced
1¼ pounds lean ground beef, browned, drained 567 g
1 (10 ounce) can cream of mushroom soup   280 g
1 (10 ounce) can vegetable beef soup   280 g

- Preheat oven to 350° (176° C).

- In large bowl, combine all ingredients plus ½ teaspoon
  each of salt and pepper and transfer to sprayed 3-quart
  (3 L) baking dish.

- Bake covered for 1 hour 30 minutes or until potatoes
  are tender.

Casserole Supper

1 (1 pound) lean ground beef   .5 kg
¼ cup white rice   60 ml
1 (10 ounce) can French onion soup   280 g
1 (3 ounce) can french-fried onion rings   84 g

- Preheat oven to 325° (162° C).

- Brown ground beef, drain and place in sprayed 7 x 11-inch
  (18 x 28 cm) baking dish. Add rice, onion soup and ½ cup
  (120 ml) water.

- Cover and bake for 40 minutes. Uncover, sprinkle
  onion rings over top and return to oven for 10 minutes.

Steak-Bake Italiano

2 pounds lean round steak	1 kg
2 teaspoons Italian herb seasoning	10 ml
1 teaspoon garlic salt	5 ml
2 (15 ounce) cans stewed tomatoes	2 (425 g)

- Preheat oven to 325° (162° C).

- Cut steak into serving-size pieces, brown in skillet and place in 9 x 13-inch (23 x 33 cm) baking dish.

- Combine herb seasoning, garlic salt and stewed tomatoes, mix well and pour over steak pieces.

- Cover and bake for 1 hour.

Easy Chili

2 pounds lean ground beef	1 kg
1 onion, chopped	
4 (16 ounce) cans chili-hot beans with liquid	4 (.5 kg)
1 (1 ounce) package chili seasoning mix	28 g
1 (46 ounce) can tomato juice	1.3 kg

- Cook beef and onion in large, heavy pan, stir until meat crumbles and drain.

- Stir in remaining ingredients. Bring mixture to a boil, reduce heat and simmer, and stir occasionally, for 2 hours.

Pinto Beef Pie

1 (1 pound) lean ground beef	.5 kg
1 onion, chopped	
2 (16 ounce) cans pinto beans with liquid	2 (.5 kg)
1 (10 ounce) can tomatoes and green chilies with liquid	280 g
1 (6 ounce) can french-fried onion rings	168 g

- Preheat oven to 350° (176° C).

- In skillet, brown beef and onion and drain.

- In 2-quart (2 L) baking dish, layer 1 can beans, beef-onion mixture and ½ can tomatoes and green chilies. Repeat layer.

- Top with onion rings and bake uncovered for 30 minutes.

Taco Pie

1½ pounds lean ground beef	.7 kg
½ green bell pepper, chopped	
1 teaspoon oil	5 ml
1 (15 ounce) can Mexican stewed tomatoes	425 g
1 tablespoon chili powder	15 ml
¼ teaspoon garlic powder	1 ml
1½ cups shredded cheddar cheese	360 ml
1 (6 ounce) package corn muffin mix	168 g
1 egg	
⅔ cup milk	160 ml

- Preheat oven to 375° (190° C).

- Brown ground beef and bell pepper in large skillet in oil and drain well.

- Add ½ teaspoon salt, tomatoes, 1 cup (240 ml) water, chili powder and garlic powder. Cook on medium heat for about 10 minutes or until most of liquid is gone.

- Pour into sprayed 9 x 13-inch (23 x 33 cm) baking dish. Sprinkle cheese on top.

- Combine corn muffin mix, egg and milk and beat well. Pour over cheese.

- Bake for 25 minutes or until corn muffin mix is light brown.

- Remove from oven and let set about 10 minutes before serving.

Simple Spaghetti Bake

8 ounces spaghetti	227 g
1 (1 pound) lean ground beef	.5 kg
1 green bell pepper, finely chopped	
1 onion, chopped	
1 (10 ounce) can tomato-bisque soup	280 g
1 (15 ounce) can tomato sauce	425 g
2 teaspoons Italian seasoning	10 ml
1 (8 ounce) can whole kernel corn, drained	227 g
1 (4 ounce) can black sliced olives, drained	114 g
1 (12 ounce) package shredded cheddar	
cheese	340 g

- Cook spaghetti according to package directions, drain and set aside.

- In skillet, cook beef, bell pepper and onion and drain.

- Add remaining ingredients, ⅓ cup (120 ml) water and ½ teaspoon (2 ml) salt and spaghetti to beef mixture and stir well. Pour into sprayed 9 x 13-inch (23 x 33 cm) baking dish and cover.

- Refrigerate 2 to 3 hours, then preheat oven to 350° (176° C).

- Bake covered for 45 minutes.

Easy Winter Warmer

*This is such a good spaghetti sauce on noodles
and is a great substitute for cream sauce.*

1 (12 ounce) package medium egg noodles	340 g
3 tablespoons butter	45 ml
1½ pounds lean ground round beef	.7 kg
1 (10 ounce) package frozen seasoning blend (chopped onions and peppers), thawed	280 g
1 (28 ounce) jar spaghetti sauce	794 g
1 (12 ounce) package shredded mozzarella cheese	340 g

- Preheat oven to 350° (176° C).

- Cook noodles according to package directions in pot of boiling water with a dab of oil and salt. Drain thoroughly, add butter and stir until butter melts.

- Brown beef and onions and peppers and drain thoroughly.

- Pour half of spaghetti sauce in bottom of sprayed 9 x 13-inch (23 x 33 cm) baking dish.

- Layer half noodles, half beef and half cheese. Repeat for second layer.

- Bake covered for about 30 minutes or until dish is hot.

Pepper Steak

1 (1¼ pound) sirloin steak, cut in strips	567 g
Seasoned salt	
1 (16 ounce) package frozen bell pepper and onion strips, thawed	.5 kg
1 (16 ounce) package cubed Mexican Velveeta® cheese	.5 kg

- Sprinkle steak with seasoned salt.
- Spray large skillet and cook steak strips for 10 minutes or until no longer pink.
- Remove steak from skillet and set aside.
- Stir in vegetables and ½ cup water and simmer vegetables for 5 minutes or until all liquid cooks out.
- Add cheese and turn heat to medium-low.
- When cheese melts, stir in steak and serve over hot, cooked rice.

Ravioli and More

1 (1 pound) lean ground beef	.5 kg
1 teaspoon garlic powder	5 ml
1 large onion, chopped	
2 zucchini squash, grated	
¼ cup (½ stick) butter	60 ml
1 (28 ounce) jar spaghetti sauce	794 g
1 (25 ounce) package cooked ravioli with portobello mushrooms	708 g
1 (12 ounce) package shredded mozzarella cheese	340 g

- Preheat oven to 350° (176° C).

- Brown ground beef in large skillet until no longer pink and drain. Add garlic powder and ½ teaspoon (2 ml) salt.

- In saucepan cook onion and zucchini in butter just until tender-crisp and stir in spaghetti sauce.

- In sprayed 9 x 13-inch baking dish, spread ½ cup (120 ml) sauce. Layer half of ravioli, half spaghetti sauce, half beef and half cheese. Repeat layers, but omit remaining cheese. Cover and bake for 35 minutes.

- Uncover and sprinkle remaining cheese. Let stand 10 minutes before serving.

Asian Beef and Noodles

1¼ pounds ground beef	567 g
2 (3 ounce) packages Oriental-flavored ramen noodles	2 (84 g)
1 (16 ounce) package frozen oriental stir-fry vegetable mixture	.5 kg
½ teaspoon ground ginger	2 ml
3 tablespoons thinly sliced green onions	45 ml

- In large skillet, brown ground beef and drain.

- Add ½ cup (120 ml) water, a little salt and pepper, simmer 10 minutes and transfer to separate bowl.

- In same skillet, combine 2 cups (480 ml) water, vegetables, noodles (broken up), ginger and both seasoning packets.

- Bring to a boil and reduce heat.

- Cover, simmer 3 minutes or until noodles are tender and stir occasionally.

- Return beef to skillet and stir in green onions. Serve right from skillet.

Shepherds' Pie

1 pound lean ground beef	.5 kg
1 (1 ounce) packet taco seasoning mix	28 g
1 cup shredded cheddar cheese	240 ml
1 (11 ounce) can whole kernel corn, drained	312 g
2 cups instant mashed potatoes, prepared	480 ml

- Preheat oven to 350° (176° C).

- In skillet, brown beef, cook 10 minutes and drain.

- Add taco seasoning and ¾ cup (180 ml) water and cook another 5 minutes. Spoon beef mixture into 8-inch (20 cm) baking pan and sprinkle cheese on top.

- Sprinkle with corn and spread mashed potatoes over top. Bake for 25 minutes or until top is golden.

Smothered Beef Patties

1½ pounds ground beef	.7 kg
½ cup chili sauce	120 ml
½ cup round, buttery cracker crumbs	120 ml
1 (14 ounce) can beef broth	396 g

- Combine beef, chili sauce and cracker crumbs and form into 5 or 6 patties.

- In skillet, brown patties, pour beef broth over patties and bring to a boil. Reduce heat, cover and simmer for 40 minutes.

Potato-Beef Bake

This is really good sprinkled with 1 cup shredded cheddar cheese.

1 pound ground beef	.5 kg
1 (10 ounce) can sloppy Joe sauce	280 g
1 (10 ounce) can fiesta nacho cheese soup	280 g
1 (32 ounce) package frozen hash browned potatoes, thawed	1 kg

- Preheat oven to 400° (204° C).

- In skillet, cook beef over medium heat until no longer pink and drain.

- Add sloppy Joe sauce and cheese soup to beef and mix well.

- Place hash browns in sprayed 9 x 13-inch (23 x 33 cm) baking dish and top with beef mixture.

- Cover and bake for 25 minutes.

- Uncover and bake additional 10 minutes.

Delicious Meatloaf

1½ pounds lean ground beef	.7 kg
⅔ cup dry Italian-seasoned breadcrumbs	160 ml
1 (10 ounce) can golden mushroom soup, divided	280 g
2 eggs, beaten	
2 tablespoons butter	30 ml

- Preheat oven to 350° (176° C).

- Mix beef, breadcrumbs, half mushroom soup and eggs thoroughly. In baking pan, shape firmly into 8 x 4-inch (20 x 10 cm) loaf and bake for 45 minutes.

- In small saucepan, mix butter, remaining soup and ¼ cup (60 ml) water, heat thoroughly and serve sauce over meatloaf.

Spanish Meatloaf

1½ pounds lean ground beef	.7 kg
1 (16 ounce) can Spanish rice	.5 kg
1 egg, beaten	
¾ cup round, buttery cracker crumbs	180 ml
Chunky salsa	

- Preheat oven to 350° (176° C).

- Combine beef, rice, egg and cracker crumbs and shape into loaf in sprayed pan. Bake for 1 hour. Serve meatloaf topped with salsa.

Baked Onion-Mushroom Steak

1½ pounds (½ inch) thick round steak   .7 kg/1.2 cm
1 (10 ounce) can cream of mushroom soup   280 g
1 (1 ounce) packet dry onion soup mix   28 g

- Preheat oven to 325° (162° C).
- Place steak in sprayed 9 x 13-inch (23 x 33 cm) baking dish and sprinkle with a little salt and pepper.
- Pour mushroom soup and ½ cup (120 ml) water over steak and sprinkle with onion soup mix.
- Cover and bake for 2 hours.

Smothered Beef Steak

2 pounds lean round steak   1 kg
1 cup rice   240 ml
1 (14 ounce) can beef broth   396 g
1 green bell pepper, chopped

- Cut steak into serving-size pieces and brown in very large skillet.
- Add rice, beef broth, bell pepper and 1 cup (240 ml) water to skillet and bring to a boil.
- Reduce heat, cover and simmer for 1 hour.

Red Wine Round Steak

2 pounds (¾ inch) thick round steak	1 kg/1.8 cm
1 (1 ounce) packet dry onion soup mix	28 g
1 cup dry red wine	240 ml
1 (4 ounce) can sliced mushrooms	114 g

- Preheat oven to 325° (162° C).

- Remove all fat from steak and cut into serving-size pieces. Brown meat in skillet with a little oil. When browned on both sides, place in sprayed 9 x 13-inch (23 x 33 cm) baking dish.

- In frying pan, combine soup mix, wine, mushrooms and 1 cup (240 ml) hot water and pour over steak. Cover and bake for 1 hour 20 minutes or until steak is tender.

Smothered Steak

1 (2 pound) round steak	1 kg
1 (10 ounce) can golden mushroom soup	280 g
1 (1 ounce) packet dry onion soup mix	28 g
⅔ cup milk	160 ml

- Preheat oven to 325° (162° C). Cut steak into serving-size pieces and place in sprayed 9 x 13-inch (23 x 33 cm) baking pan.

- In saucepan, combine mushroom soup, soup mix and milk. Heat just enough to mix well and pour over steak. Seal with foil and bake for 1 hour.

Lean Mean Round Steak

Flour	
1 teaspoon paprika	5 ml
2 pounds lean round steak, cut into strips	1kg
2 tablespoons oil	30 ml
1 cup chopped onions	240 ml
½ cup chopped green bell pepper	120 ml
2 (15 ounce) cans Mexican stewed tomatoes	2 (425 g)
2 (8 ounce) cans tomato sauce	2 (227 g)
1 tablespoon chili powder	15 ml
Shredded cheddar cheese	
Fresh cilantro	

- Combine flour, paprika and a little salt and pepper in bowl. Dredge steak strips in flour and set aside.

- Heat oil in large, heavy skillet over medium heat. Brown meat and add onions, bell peppers, tomatoes, tomato sauce, chili powder and 1 cup (240 ml) water. Reduce heat to medium-low, cover and simmer for 1 hour.

- To serve, arrange steak on hot, ovenproof serving platter and cover with sauce. Sprinkle shredded cheese on top.

- Place under broiler for 1 to 2 minutes or until cheese melts. Garnish with fresh cilantro.

- Serve over hot, cooked rice. Serves 6 to 8.

Roasted Garlic Steak

2 (15 ounce) cans tomato soup with roasted
   garlic and herbs   2 (425 g)
½ cup prepared Italian salad dressing   120 ml
1½ pounds (¾ inch) thick boneless beef
   sirloin steak   .7 kg/1.8 cm

- In saucepan, combine soup, salad dressing and ⅓ cup (80 ml) water.

- Broil steaks to desired doneness. (Allow 15 minutes for medium.) Turn once and brush often with sauce.

- Heat remaining sauce to serve with steak.

Pot Roast

4 - 6 pound chuck roast   1.8 kg
1 (10 ounce) can French onion soup   280 g
1 (1 ounce) packet dry onion soup mix   28 g
4 - 6 potatoes, peeled, quartered

- Preheat oven to 350° (176° C).

- Place roast on large sheet of heavy-duty foil.

- Combine soup and soup mix and spread over roast.

- Add potatoes and secure edges of foil tightly.

- Bake for 3 to 4 hours.

Slow Cookin', Good Tastin' Brisket

½ cup hickory-flavored liquid smoke	120 ml
1 (4 - 5 pound) beef brisket	1.8 kg
1 (5 ounce) bottle Worcestershire sauce	143 g
¾ cup barbecue sauce	180 ml

- Preheat oven to 275° (135° C).

- Pour liquid smoke over brisket, cover and chill overnight.

- Drain and pour Worcestershire sauce over brisket.

- Cover and bake for 6 to 7 hours.

- Cover with barbecue sauce and bake uncovered, for additional 30 minutes.

- Slice very thinly across grain.

Next-Day Beef

1 (5 - 6 pound) trimmed beef brisket	2.2 kg
1 (1 ounce) packet dry onion soup mix	28 g
1 (10 ounce) bottle steak sauce	280 g
1 (12 ounce) bottle barbecue sauce	340 g

- Preheat oven to 325° (162° C).

- Place brisket, cut side up, in roasting pan.

- In bowl, combine onion soup mix, steak and barbecue sauces and pour over brisket.

- Cover and cook for 4 to 5 hours or until tender.

- Remove brisket from pan, pour off drippings and chill both, separately, overnight.

- The next day, trim all fat from meat, slice and reheat.

- Skim fat off drippings, reheat and serve sauce over brisket.

Deluxe Dinner Nachos

Nachos:

1 (14 ounce) package tortilla chips, divided	396 g
1 (8 ounce) package shredded Velveeta® cheese, divided	227 g
1 (8 ounce) can chopped jalapenos, divided	227 g

Deluxe Nacho Topping:

1 (11 ounce) can Mexicorn® with liquid	312 g
1 (15 ounce) can jalapeno pinto beans, drained	425 g
2 cups skinned, chopped rotisserie chicken	480 ml
1 bunch fresh green onions, chopped	

- Place about three-quarters of tortilla chips in bottom of sprayed baking dish. Sprinkle half cheese and about 3 jalapenos on top. Heat at 400ϒ (204° C) just until cheese melts.

- Combine corn, beans and rotisserie chicken in saucepan. Heat over medium heat, stirring constantly, until mixture is hot. Spoon mixture over nachos, place dish in oven and heat for about 10 minutes.

- Sprinkle remaining cheese and green onions over top and serve immediately. Garnish with remaining jalapenos, remaining tortillas and salsa.

Chucky Clucky Casserole

1 (16 ounce) package frozen broccoli spears	.5 kg
3 cups cooked, diced chicken	710 ml
1 (10 ounce) can cream of chicken soup	280 g
2 tablespoons milk	30 ml
⅓ cup mayonnaise	80 ml
2 teaspoons lemon juice	10 ml
3 tablespoons butter, melted	45 ml
1 cup breadcrumbs or cracker crumbs	240 ml
⅓ cup shredded cheddar cheese	80 ml

- Preheat oven to 350° (176° C).

- Cook broccoli according to package directions and drain. Place broccoli in sprayed 9 x 13-inch (23 x 33 cm) glass baking dish. Sprinkle 1 teaspoon (5 ml) salt over broccoli and cover with diced chicken.

- In saucepan, combine soup, milk, mayonnaise, lemon juice and ¼ teaspoon (1 ml) pepper. Heat just enough to dilute soup a little and pour over chicken.

- Mix melted butter, breadcrumbs and cheese and sprinkle over soup mixture. Bake uncovered for 30 minutes or until mixture is hot and bubbly.

Chicken Chow Mein

3½ cups cooked, cubed chicken breasts	830 ml
2 (10 ounce) cans cream of chicken soup	2 (280 g)
2 (15 ounce) cans chop suey vegetables, drained	2 (425 g)
1 (8 ounce) can sliced water chestnuts, drained	227 g
¾ cup chopped cashew nuts	180 ml
1 green bell pepper, chopped	
1 onion, chopped	
1 cup chopped celery	240 ml
¼ teaspoon hot sauce	1 ml
1¼ cups chow mein noodles	300 ml

- Preheat oven to 350° (176° C).

- Combine chicken, soup, vegetables, water chestnuts, cashew nuts, green pepper, onion, celery and hot sauce in large bowl. Stir to mix well.

- Spoon into sprayed 9 x 13-inch (23 x 33 cm) baking dish. Sprinkle chow mein noodles over top of casserole.

- Bake uncovered for 35 minutes or until it bubbles at edges of casserole. Let set 5 minutes before serving.

Chicken Spaghetti

3 chicken breasts, boiled
1 (10 ounce) can tomatoes and green chilies   280 g
1 (10 ounce) can cream of mushroom soup   280 g
1 (8 ounce) package shredded cheddar cheese   227 g
1 (8 ounce) package shredded Velveeta® cheese   227 g
1 (12 ounce) package spaghetti   340 g

- Preheat oven to 350° (176° C).

- Shred cooked chicken into large bowl. Add tomatoes, soup, cheddar cheese and velveeta cheese. Boil spaghetti according to package directions and drain.

- Add to chicken mixture; mix well. Pour into 3-quart (3 L) baking dish and bake for 35 minutes.

Alfredo Chicken

5 - 6 boneless, skinless chicken breast halves
1 (16 ounce) package frozen broccoli florets,
   thawed   .5 kg
1 sweet red bell pepper, seeded, chopped
1 (16 ounce) jar alfredo sauce   .5 kg

- Preheat oven to 325° (162° C).

- Brown and cook chicken breasts in large skillet with a little oil until juices run clear. Transfer to sprayed 9 x 13-inch (23 x 33 cm) baking dish.

- Microwave broccoli according to package directions and drain. Spoon broccoli and bell pepper over chicken.

- In small saucepan, heat alfredo sauce with ¼ cup (60 ml) water. Pour over chicken and vegetables. Cover and cook 15 to 20 minutes.

TIP: This chicken-broccoli dish can be "dressed up" a bit by sprinkling shredded parmesan cheese on top after casserole bakes.

Quickie Russian Chicken

This is great when you don't have time to cook.

6 boneless, skinless chicken breast halves
1 (8 ounce) bottle Russian salad dressing   227 g
1 (5 ounce) jar apricot preserves   143 g
1 (1 ounce) packet dry onion soup mix   28 g

- Preheat oven to 350° (176° C).

- Place chicken breasts in sprayed, shallow baking dish.

- Combine dressing, apricot preserves, onion soup mix and ¼ cup (60 ml) water in saucepan and bring to a slow boil. Remove from heat and pour over chicken.

- Cover dish with foil and bake for 1 hour. Remove foil, baste with sauce and bake uncovered for additional 30 minutes. Serve immediately.

Aztec Creamy Salsa Chicken

6 boneless, skinless chicken breast halves
Oil
1 (1 ounce) packet dry taco seasoning mix   28 g
1 (16 ounce) jar salsa   .5 kg
1 (8 ounce) carton sour cream   227 g

- Preheat oven to 350° (176° C).

- Brown chicken breasts in skillet and transfer to sprayed 9 x 13-inch (23 x 33 cm) baking dish. Sprinkle taco seasoning over chicken and top with salsa.

- Cover and bake for 35 minutes.

- Remove chicken to serving plates. Add sour cream to juices in pan, stir well and microwave on HIGH for about 2 minutes. Stir pan juices and sour cream for sauce to serve over chicken.

Finger Lickin' BBQ Chicken

1 (2 pound) chicken, quartered	1 kg
½ cup ketchup	120 ml
¼ cup (½ stick) butter, melted	60 ml
2 tablespoons sugar	30 ml
1 tablespoon mustard	15 ml
½ teaspoon minced garlic	2 ml
¼ cup lemon juice	60 ml
¼ cup white vinegar	60 ml
¼ cup Worcestershire sauce	60 ml

- Preheat oven to 325° (162° C).

- Sprinkle chicken quarters with salt and pepper and brown in skillet. Place in large sprayed baking pan.

- Combine ketchup, butter, sugar, mustard, garlic, lemon juice, vinegar and Worcestershire. Pour over chicken, cover and bake for 50 minutes.

Parmesan Chicken Breasts

6 boneless, skinless chicken breast halves
1½ cups dry breadcrumbs — 360 ml
½ cup grated parmesan cheese — 120 ml
1 teaspoon dried basil — 5 ml
½ teaspoon garlic powder — 2 ml
1 (8 ounce) carton sour cream — 227 g

- Preheat oven to 325° (162° C).

- Flatten chicken to ½-inch (1.2 cm) thickness. Combine breadcrumbs, parmesan cheese, basil and garlic powder in shallow dish.

- Dip chicken in sour cream, coat with crumb mixture and place (so chicken breasts do not touch) in sprayed 10 x 15-inch (25 x 38 cm) baking dish.

- Bake uncovered for 50 to 60 minutes or until golden brown.

An easy way to get seasonings and spices to stick to chicken and roasts is to place them on plastic wrap, season well on all sides and roll meat in plastic wrap. By pressing seasonings into meat, they are more likely to stay on all sides. Remove wrap and cook.

Chile-Chicken Roll-Ups

8 boneless, skinless chicken breast halves
2 (4 ounce) cans diced green chilies   2 (114 g)
1 (8 ounce) package shredded cheddar cheese   227 g
½ cup (1 stick) butter, melted   120 ml
2 cups crushed tortilla chips   480 ml

- Place each chicken breast on wax paper, flatten to about ¼-inch (.6 cm) thickness with rolling pin or mallet and season with 1 teaspoon (5 ml) salt and ½ teaspoon (2 ml) pepper.

- Place diced green chilies and a little cheese evenly in center of each chicken breast. Carefully roll each chicken breast so no chilies or cheese seep out and secure with toothpicks.

- Place each chicken in small casserole dish and chill several hours or overnight. When ready to bake, roll each chicken breast in melted butter and crushed tortilla chips.

- Bake at 350° (176° C) for about 25 to 30 minutes or until tender.

Chicken Quesadillas

3 boneless, skinless chicken breast halves, cubed
1 (10 ounce) can cheddar cheese soup   280 g
⅔ cup chunky salsa   160 ml
10 flour tortillas

- Preheat oven to 400° (204° C).

- Cook chicken in skillet until juices evaporate and stir often. Add soup and salsa and heat thoroughly.

- Spread about ⅓ cup (80 ml) soup mixture on half tortilla to within ½-inch (1.2 cm) of edge. Moisten edge with water, fold over and seal. Place tortillas on 2 baking sheets. Bake for 5 to 6 minutes.

Cola Chicken

4 - 6 boneless, skinless chicken breast halves
1 cup ketchup   240 ml
1 cup cola   240 ml
2 tablespoons Worcestershire sauce   30 ml

- Preheat oven to 350° (176° C).

- Place chicken in 9 x 13-inch (23 x 33 cm) baking dish and sprinkle with salt and pepper.

- Mix ketchup, cola and Worcestershire sauce and pour over chicken. Cover and bake for 50 minutes.

Crunchy Chip Chicken

1½ cups crushed sour cream potato chips	360 ml
1 tablespoon dried parsley	15 ml
1 egg, beaten	
1 tablespoon Worcestershire sauce	15 ml
4 large boneless, skinless chicken breast halves	
¼ cup oil	60 ml

- In shallow bowl, combine potato chips and parsley. In another shallow bowl, combine beaten egg, Worcestershire and 1 tablespoon water.

- Dip chicken pieces in egg mixture and dredge chicken in potato chip mixture. Heat oil in heavy skillet and fry chicken pieces in skillet for about 10 minutes.

- Turn each piece over and cook additional 10 minutes until golden brown or until juices run clear.

Cranberry Chicken

6 boneless, skinless chicken breast halves
1 (16 ounce) can whole cranberry sauce   .5 kg
1 large tart apple, peeled, chopped
⅓ cup chopped walnuts   80 ml
1 teaspoon curry powder   5 ml

■ Place chicken in sprayed 9 x 13-inch (23 x 33 cm)
  baking pan and bake uncovered at 350° (176° C) for
  20 minutes. Combine cranberry sauce, apple, walnuts
  and curry powder and spoon over chicken.

■ Bake uncovered for additional 25 minutes or until
  chicken juices run clear.

Spicy Chicken and Rice

3 cups cooked sliced chicken   710 ml
2 cups cooked brown rice   480 ml
1 (10 ounce) can fiesta nacho cheese soup   280 g
1 (10 ounce) can chopped tomatoes and
  green chilies   280 g

■ Preheat oven to 350° (176° C).

■ Combine chicken, rice, cheese soup, tomatoes and
  green chilies and mix well. Spoon mixture into
  sprayed 3-quart (3L) baking dish.

■ Cook covered for 45 minutes.

Ranch Chicken

½ cup parmesan cheese	120 ml
1½ cups corn flakes	360 ml
1 (1 ounce) packet dry ranch-style salad dressing mix	28
2 pounds chicken drumsticks	1 kg
½ cup (1 stick) butter, melted	120 ml

- Preheat oven to 350° (176° C).

- Combine cheese, corn flakes and dressing mix.

- Dip washed, dried chicken in melted butter and dredge in corn flake mixture.

- Bake uncovered for 50 minutes or until golden brown.

Sunday Chicken

5 - 6 boneless, skinless chicken breast halves	
½ cup sour cream	120 ml
¼ cup soy sauce	60 ml
1 (10 ounce) can French onion soup	280 g

- Preheat oven to 350° (176° C). Place chicken in sprayed 9 x 13-inch (23 x 33 cm) baking dish.

- In saucepan, combine sour cream, soy sauce and soup and heat just enough to mix well. Pour over chicken breasts.

- Bake covered for 55 minutes.

Chicken and Wild Rice Special

1 (6 ounce) package long grain-wild rice mix   168 g
4 - 5 boneless, skinless chicken breast halves
2 (10 ounce) cans French onion soup   2 (280 g)
1 red and 1 green bell pepper, julienned

- In saucepan, cook rice according to package directions and keep warm. In large skillet with a little oil over medium-high heat, brown chicken breasts on both sides.

- Add soups, ¾ cup (180 ml) water and bell peppers. Reduce heat to medium-low, cover and cook 15 minutes.

- To serve, place rice on serving platter with chicken breasts on top. Serve sauce in gravy boat to pour over chicken and rice.

TIP: For a thicker sauce, spoon 2 or 3 tablespoons (30 ml) sauce in small bowl and stir in 2 tablespoons (30 ml) flour. Mix well and stir in onion soup. Heat and stir constantly until sauce thickens.

Party Chicken Breasts

6 - 8 boneless, skinless chicken breast halves
8 strips bacon
1 (2.5 ounce) jar dried beef   70 g
1 (10 ounce) can cream of chicken soup   280 g
1 (8 ounce) carton sour cream   227 g

- Preheat oven to 325° (162° C).

- Wrap each chicken breast with 1 strip bacon and secure with toothpicks.

- Place dried beef in bottom of large, shallow baking pan and top with chicken. Heat soup and sour cream, just enough to pour over chicken. Bake uncovered for 1 hour.

Lemonade Chicken

6 boneless, skinless chicken breast halves
1 (6 ounce) can frozen lemonade, thawed   168 g
⅓ cup soy sauce   80 ml
1 teaspoon garlic powder   5 ml

- Preheat oven to 350° (176° C).

- Place chicken in sprayed 9 x 13-inch (23 x 33 cm) baking dish. Combine lemonade, soy sauce and garlic powder and pour over chicken.

- Cover with foil and bake for 45 minutes. Uncover, pour juices over chicken and cook additional 10 minutes.

Dad's Best Smoked Chicken

3 whole chickens, cut in half
½ cup (1 stick) butter   120 ml
2 teaspoons Worcestershire sauce   10 ml
2 dashes hot sauce
2 tablespoons lemon juice   30 ml
½ teaspoon garlic salt   2 ml
1 (12 ounce) can lemon-lime carbonated drink   340 g

■ Sprinkle chickens with pepper and leave at room
   temperature for 1 hour. In small saucepan, melt
   butter and add Worcestershire sauce, hot sauce, lemon
   juice and garlic salt and add lemon-lime carbonated
   drink.

■ Cook chickens over low charcoal fire with hickory or
   mesquite chips around sides of fire. Turn often and
   baste with sauce mixture several times.

■ When chicken is done (about 60 minutes), baste once
   more to keep chicken moist.

Grilled Chicken Cordon Bleu

6 boneless, skinless chicken breast halves
6 slices Swiss cheese
6 thin slices deli ham
3 tablespoons oil   45 ml
1 cup seasoned breadcrumbs   240 ml

- Flatten chicken to ¼-inch (.6 cm) thickness and place
  1 slice cheese and ham on each piece of chicken to
  within ¼-inch (.6 cm) of edges.

- Fold in half and secure with toothpicks. Brush chicken
  with oil and roll in breadcrumbs. Grill, covered, over
  medium heat for 15 to 18 minutes or until juices run clear.

Italian Chicken and Rice

3 boneless, chicken breasts halves, cut into strips
1 (14 ounce) can chicken broth seasoned
   with Italian herbs   396 g
¾ cup rice   180 ml
¼ cup grated parmesan cheese   60 ml

- Cook chicken in non-stick skillet until brown, stirring
  often, and set aside.

- Add broth and rice to skillet and heat to boil. Cover
  and simmer over low heat for 25 minutes. (Add water
  if needed.) Stir in cheese and return chicken to pan.
  Cover and cook for 5 minutes or until done.

Lemony Chicken and Noodles

1 (8 ounce) package wide egg noodles	227 g
1 (10 ounce) package frozen sugar snap peas, thawed	280 g
1 (14 ounce) can chicken broth	396 g
1 teaspoon fresh grated lemon peel	5 ml
2 cups cubed, skinless rotisserie chicken meat	480 ml
½ cup whipping cream	120 ml

- In large saucepan with boiling water, cook noodles according to package directions, but add snap peas to noodles 1 minute before noodles are done. Drain and return to saucepan.

- Add chicken broth, lemon peel, chicken pieces and ½ teaspoon (2 ml) each of salt and pepper. Heat, stirring constantly, until thoroughly hot.

- Over low heat, gently stir in heavy cream. Serve hot.

Sweet-and-Sour Chicken

6 - 8 boneless, skinless chicken breast halves
Oil
1 (1 ounce) packet dry onion soup mix   28 g
1 (6 ounce) can frozen orange juice concentrate,
    thawed   168 g

- Preheat oven to 350° (176° C).

- Brown chicken in a little oil or butter and place in sprayed 9 x 13-inch (23 x 33 cm) baking dish.

- In small bowl, combine soup mix, orange juice and ⅔ cup (160 ml) water, mix well and pour over chicken.

- Bake uncovered for 45 to 50 minutes.

More statistical studies are finding that family meals play a significant role in childhood development. Children who eat with their families four or more nights per week are healthier, make better grades in school, score higher on aptitude tests and are less likely to have problems with drugs.

Stir-Fry Chicken Spaghetti

1 (1 pound) boneless, skinless chicken breast halves	.5 kg
1½ cups sliced mushrooms	360 ml
1½ cups bell pepper strips	360 ml
1 cup sweet-and-sour stir-fry sauce	240 ml
1 (16 ounce) package cooked spaghetti	.5 kg
¼ cup (½ stick) butter	60 ml

- Season chicken with a little salt and pepper and cut into thin slices. Brown chicken slices in large skillet with a little oil and cook for 5 minutes on medium-low heat. Transfer to plate and set aside.

- In same skillet with a little more oil, stir-fry mushrooms and bell pepper strips for 5 minutes. Add chicken strips and sweet-and-sour sauce and stir until ingredients are hot.

- While spaghetti is still hot, drain well, add butter and stir until butter melts. Place in large bowl and toss with chicken mixture. Serve hot.

Hawaiian Chicken

2 small whole chickens, quartered
Flour
Oil
1 (20 ounce) can sliced pineapple with juice   567 g
2 bell peppers, cut in strips

- Wash and pat chicken dry with paper towels.

- Coat chicken with a little salt and pepper and flour, brown in oil and place in shallow pan. Drain pineapple into 2-cup (480 ml) measure, add enough water (or orange juice, if you have it) to make 1½ cups (360 ml) liquid and set aside.

Sauce for Hawaiian Chicken:

1 cup sugar	240 ml
3 tablespoons cornstarch	45 ml
¾ cup vinegar	180 ml
1 tablespoon lemon juice	15 ml
1 tablespoon soy sauce	15 ml
2 teaspoons chicken bouillon granules	10 ml

- Preheat oven to 350° (176° C). In medium saucepan, combine reserved 1½ cups (360 ml) juice with sauce ingredients.

- Bring to boil and stir constantly until thick and clear, then pour over chicken. Bake covered 40 minutes.

- Place pineapple slices and bell pepper on top of chicken and bake additional 10 minutes. Serve on white rice.

Chile Pepper Chicken

5 boneless, skinless chicken breast halves
1 (1 ounce) package hot-and-spicy coating
   mixture   28 g
1 (4 ounce) can chopped green chilies   114 g
Chunky salsa

- Preheat oven to 375° (190 C).

- Dredge chicken in coating mixture and place in
  sprayed 9 x 13-inch (23 x 33 cm) baking dish.

- Bake for 25 minutes. Remove from oven, spread green
  chilies over chicken breasts and return to oven for
  5 minutes. Serve with salsa over each chicken breast.

Apricot Chicken

1 cup apricot preserves   240 ml
1 (8 ounce) bottle Catalina salad dressing   227 g
1 (1 ounce) packet dry onion soup mix   28 g
6 - 8 boneless, skinless chicken breast halves

- Preheat oven to 325° (162° C).

- Combine apricot preserves, salad dressing and soup
  mix. Place chicken breasts in large, sprayed baking dish
  and pour apricot mixture over chicken. (For a change
  of pace, use Russian dressing instead of Catalina).

- Bake uncovered for 1 hour 20 minutes. Serve over rice.

Catalina Chicken

6 - 8 boneless, skinless chicken breast halves
1 (8 ounce) bottle Catalina salad dressing   227 g
1½ cups crushed cracker crumbs   360 ml

- Preheat oven to 350° (176° C).

- Marinate chicken breasts in dressing for 3 to 4 hours
  and discard marinade. Combine 1 teaspoon (5 ml)
  pepper and cracker crumbs.

- Dip each chicken breast in crumb mixture and place in
  large, sprayed baking dish. Bake uncovered for 1 hour.

Crispy Nutty Chicken

⅓ cup dry-roasted peanuts, minced   80 ml
1 cup corn flake crumbs   240 ml
½ cup ranch-style buttermilk salad dressing   120 ml
6 boneless, skinless chicken breast halves

- Preheat oven to 350° (176° C).

- Combine peanuts and crumbs on wax paper.

- Pour dressing into pie pan, dip each piece of chicken
  in dressing and roll chicken in crumb mixture to coat.

- Arrange chicken in shallow 9 x 13-inch (23 x 33 cm)
  baking dish.

- Bake uncovered for 50 minutes or until light brown.

One-Dish Chicken Bake

1 (1 ounce) packet dry vegetable soup mix	28 g
1 (6 ounce) package chicken stuffing mix	168 g
4 boneless, skinless chicken breast halves	
1 (10 ounce) can cream of mushroom soup	280 g
⅓ cup sour cream	80 ml

- Preheat oven to 375° (190° C).

- Toss soup mix, stuffing mix and 1⅔ cups water and set aside.

- Place chicken in sprayed 9 x 13-inch (23 x 33 cm) baking dish.

- Mix soup and sour cream in saucepan over low heat just enough to pour over chicken and spoon stuffing mixture evenly over top.

- Bake uncovered for 40 minutes.

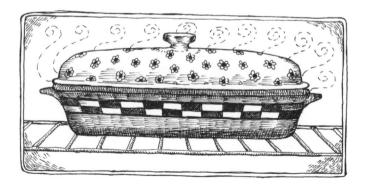

Favorite Chicken Breasts

6 - 8 boneless, skinless chicken breast halves
1 (10 ounce) can golden mushroom soup   280 g
1 cup white wine or white cooking wine   240 ml
1 (8 ounce) carton sour cream   227 g

- Place chicken breasts in large, shallow baking pan, sprinkle with a little salt and pepper and bake uncovered at 350° (176° C) for 30 minutes.

- In saucepan, combine soup, wine and sour cream and heat just enough to mix well.

- Remove chicken from oven and cover with soup mixture.

- Reduce heat to 300° (148°C) and return to oven for additional 30 minutes. Baste twice.

- Serve over rice.

Chicken Bake

8 boneless, skinless chicken breast halves
8 slices Swiss cheese
1 (10 ounce) can cream of chicken soup 280 g
1 (8 ounce) box chicken stuffing mix   227 g

- Preheat oven to 325° (162° C).

- Flatten each chicken breast with rolling pin and place in sprayed 9 x 13-inch (23 x 33 cm) baking dish.

- Place cheese slices over chicken.

- Combine chicken soup and ½ cup (120 ml) water and pour over chicken.

- Prepare stuffing mix according to package directions and sprinkle over chicken.

- Bake uncovered for 1 hour.

Mozzarella Cutlets

4 boneless, skinless chicken breast halves
1 cup dry Italian-seasoned breadcrumbs   240 ml
1 cup prepared spaghetti sauce   240 ml
4 slices mozzarella cheese

- Preheat oven to 350° (176° C).

- Pound each chicken breast to flatten slightly.

- Coat chicken well in breadcrumbs and arrange in sprayed 9 x 13-inch (23 x 33 cm) baking dish.

- Spread quarter of sauce over each portion.

- Place 1 slice cheese over each and garnish with remaining breadcrumbs.

- Bake uncovered for 45 minutes.

It is best to marinate whole chickens overnight. Boneless breast halves take up to 3 hours to reach full flavor.

Jiffy Chicken

8 boneless, skinless chicken breast halves	
¾ cup mayonnaise	180 ml
2 cups crushed corn flakes	480 ml
½ cup grated parmesan cheese	120 ml

- Preheat oven to 325° (162° C).

- Sprinkle chicken breasts with a little salt and pepper.

- Dip chicken in mayonnaise and spread over chicken with brush.

- Combine corn flake crumbs and cheese and dip chicken in corn flake mixture until it coats completely.

- Place chicken in sprayed 9 x 13-inch (23 x 33 cm) glass baking dish and bake uncovered for 1 hour.

Look for baking dishes with lids. Any leftovers can be refrigerated right in the pan they were baked in and clean-up is a snap!

Honey-Baked Chicken

2 whole chickens, quartered
½ cup (1 stick) butter, melted   120 ml
⅔ cup honey   160 ml
¼ cup dijon-style mustard   60 ml
1 teaspoon curry powder   5 ml

- Preheat oven to 350° (176° C).

- Place chicken pieces skin side up in large, shallow baking dish and sprinkle with a little salt.

- Combine butter, honey, mustard and curry powder and pour over chicken.

- Bake uncovered for 1 hour 5 minutes and baste every 20 minutes.

Party Chicken Breasts

6 - 8 boneless, skinless chicken breast halves
8 strips bacon
1 (2.5 ounce) jar dried beef   70 g
1 (10 ounce) can cream of chicken soup   280 g
1 (8 ounce) carton sour cream   227 g

- Preheat oven to 325° (162° C).

- Wrap each chicken breast with 1 strip bacon and secure with toothpicks.

- Place dried beef in bottom of large, shallow baking pan and place chicken on top.

- Heat soup and sour cream just enough to pour over chicken.

- Cover chicken with soup mixture and bake uncovered for 1 hour.

Always cook with thicker slices of bacon. Thin strips will fall apart when stretched around a chicken breast half. Don't forget to tell your guests that you used toothpicks to secure the meat.

Bacon-Wrapped Chicken

6 boneless, skinless chicken breast halves
1 (8 ounce) carton whipped cream cheese
   with onion and chives   227 g
Butter
6 bacon strips

- Preheat oven to 375° (190° C).

- Flatten chicken to ½-inch thickness and spread 3 tablespoons (45 ml) cream cheese over each piece.

- Dot with butter and sprinkle with a little salt, roll and wrap each with 1 bacon strip.

- Place seam-side down in sprayed 9 x 13-inch (23 x 33 cm) baking dish and bake uncovered for 40 to 45 minutes or until juices run clear.

- To brown, broil 6 inches (15 cm) from heat for about 3 minutes or until bacon is crisp.

Broccoli-Cheese Chicken

4 boneless, skinless chicken breast halves
1 tablespoon butter   15 ml
1 (10 ounce) can broccoli-cheese soup   280 g
1 (10 ounce) package frozen broccoli spears   280 g
⅓ cup milk   80 ml

- In skillet, cook chicken in butter for 15 minutes or until brown on both sides, remove and set aside.

- In same skillet, combine soup, broccoli, milk and a little black pepper and heat to boiling, return chicken to skillet and reduce heat to low.

- Cover and cook additional 25 minutes or until chicken is no longer pink and broccoli is tender. Serve over rice.

Asparagus-Cheese Chicken

1 tablespoon butter	15 ml
4 boneless, skinless chicken breast halves	
1 (10 ounce) can broccoli-cheese soup	280 g
1 (10 ounce) package frozen asparagus cuts	280 g
⅓ cup milk	80 ml

- In skillet, heat butter and cook chicken for 10 to 15 minutes or until brown on both sides.

- Remove chicken and set aside.

- In same skillet, combine soup, asparagus and milk and heat to a boil.

- Return chicken to skillet, reduce heat to low, cover and cook additional 25 minutes until chicken is no longer pink and asparagus is tender.

Cheesy Chicken and Potatoes

1 (20 ounce) package frozen hash browns with peppers and onions, thawed	567 g
1 tablespoon minced garlic	15 ml
2 - 2½ cups bite-size chunks rotisserie chicken	480 ml
1 bunch green onions, sliced	
1 cup shredded cheddar cheese	240 ml

- Add a little oil to large skillet over medium-high heat, cook potatoes for 7 minutes and turn frequently.

- Add garlic, chicken, green onions and ⅓ cup (80 ml water and cook 5 to 6 minutes. Remove from heat and stir in cheese. Serve immediately right from skillet.

After-Thanksgiving Turkey Chili

3 pounds ground turkey	1.3 kg
½ teaspoon garlic powder	2 ml
3 tablespoons chili powder	45 ml
1 (8 ounce) can tomato sauce	227 g
Shredded cheese	

- In large saucepan, add turkey and garlic powder with 1 cup (240 ml) water. Cook over medium heat until mixture begins to fry.

- Add chili powder and tomato sauce and simmer until meat is tender. Garnish with cheese.

Pineapple-Pork Chops

6 - 8 thick, boneless pork chops
1 (6 ounce) can frozen pineapple juice
    concentrate, thawed   168 g
3 tablespoons brown sugar   45 ml
⅓ cup wine or tarragon vinegar   80 ml
⅓ cup honey   80 ml

- ■ Preheat oven to 325° (162° C). Place pork chops in a little
  oil in skillet and brown. Remove to shallow baking dish.

- ■ Combine remaining ingredients and pour over chops.
  Cook covered for about 50 minutes. Serve over hot rice.

Oven-Pork Chops

6 - 8 medium-thick pork chops
1 (10 ounce) can cream of chicken soup   280 g
3 tablespoons ketchup   45 ml
1 tablespoon Worcestershire sauce   15 ml
1 medium onion, chopped

- ■ Preheat oven to 350° (176° C). Brown pork chops in
  a little oil and season with salt and pepper. Drain and
  place in shallow baking dish.

- ■ Combine soup, ketchup, Worcestershire and onion in
  small saucepan. Heat enough to mix and pour over pork.

- ■ Bake covered for 50 minutes. Uncover last 15 minutes.

Orange Pork Chops

6 (½ inch) thick boneless pork chops	6 (1.2 cm)
2 tablespoons oil	30 ml
1⅓ cups instant rice	320 ml
1 cup orange juice	240 ml
¼ teaspoon ground ginger	1 ml
1 (10 ounce) can condensed chicken and rice soup	280 g
½ cup chopped walnuts	120 ml

- Preheat oven to 350° (176° C).

- Sprinkle a little salt and pepper over pork chops and brown in skillet with oil.

- Sprinkle rice into sprayed 7 x 11-inch (18 x 28 cm) baking dish. Add orange juice and arrange pork chops over rice.

- Add ginger to soup and stir right in can. Pour soup over pork chops.

- Sprinkle walnuts over tops of pork chops.

- Cover and bake for 25 minutes.

- Uncover and bake additional 10 minutes or until rice is tender.

Spicy Pork Chops

4 - 6 pork chops
1 large onion
1 bell pepper
1 (10 ounce) can diced tomatoes
   and green chilies   280 g

- Preheat oven to 350° (176° C).

- Brown pork chops in skillet with a little oil.

- Spray baking dish and place chops in dish.

- Cut onion and bell pepper into large chunks and place on chops.

- Pour tomato and green chilies over chops and sprinkle with 1 teaspoon (5 ml) salt.

- Bake covered for 45 minutes.

Pork Chops in Cream Gravy

4 (¼ inch) thick pork chops	4 (.6 cm)
Flour	
Oil	
2¼ cups milk	540 ml

- Trim all fat off pork chops. Dip chops in flour with a little salt and pepper. Brown pork chops on both sides in a little oil. Remove chops from skillet.

- Add about 2 tablespoons (30 ml) flour to skillet, brown lightly and stir in a little salt and pepper. Slowly stir in milk to make gravy.

- Return chops to skillet with gravy. Cover and simmer on low burner for about 40 minutes. Serve over rice.

Pork Casserole

4 - 5 potatoes, peeled, sliced	
6 pork chops	
1 (10 ounce) can fiesta nacho cheese soup	280 g
½ soup can milk	

- Preheat oven to 350° (176° C). Place 2 layers potatoes in sprayed baking dish and place pork chops on top.

- Combine cheese and milk and heat just enough to pour over chops. Bake covered for 45 minutes. Uncover and bake additional 15 minutes.

Pork Chops and Apples

Simple and delicious!

6 thick-cut pork chops
Flour
Oil
3 baking apples

- Preheat oven to 325° (162° C).

- Dip pork chops in flour and coat well.

- In skillet, brown pork chops in oil and place in sprayed 9 x 13-inch (23 x 33 cm) baking dish.

- Add ⅓ cup (80 ml) water to casserole and bake covered for 50 minutes.

- Peel, halve and seed apples and place half apple over each pork chop.

- Return to oven for 10 minutes. (Don't overcook apples.)

Oven Pork Chops

6 - 8 medium-thick pork chops
1 (10 ounce) can cream of chicken soup   280 g
3 tablespoons ketchup   45 ml
1 tablespoon Worcestershire sauce   15 ml
1 medium onion, chopped

- Preheat oven to 350° (176° C).
- Brown pork chops in a little oil, season with a little salt and pepper and place drained pork chops in shallow baking dish.
- In saucepan, combine soup, ketchup, Worcestershire and onion, heat just enough to mix and pour over pork chops.
- Bake covered for 50 minutes. Uncover for the last 15 minutes of baking time.

Tangy Pork Chops

4 - 6 pork chops
¼ cup Worcestershire sauce   60 ml
¼ cup ketchup   60 ml
½ cup honey   120 ml

- Preheat oven to 325° (162° C). In skillet, brown pork chops and remove to shallow baking dish.
- Combine Worcestershire, ketchup and honey and pour over pork chops. Cover and bake for 45 minutes.

Onion-Smothered Pork Chops

6 (½ inch) thick pork chops	6 (1.2 cm)
1 tablespoon oil	15 ml
2 tablespoons butter	30 ml
1 onion, chopped	
1 (10 ounce) can cream of onion soup	280 g

- Preheat oven to 325° (162° C).

- In skillet, brown pork chops in oil, simmer about 10 minutes and place pork chops in sprayed shallow baking pan.

- In same skillet, add butter and saute chopped onion. (Pan juices are brown from pork chops so onions will be brown from juices already in skillet.)

- Add onion soup and ½ cup (120 ml) water and stir well. (Sauce will have a nice, light brown color.)

- Pour onion mixture over pork chops. Cover bake for 40 minutes and serve over brown rice.

Peachy Glazed Ham

1 (15 ounce) can sliced peaches in light syrup
   with juice   425 g
2 tablespoons dark brown sugar   30 ml
2 teaspoons dijon-style mustard   10 ml
1 (1 pound) center-cut ham slice   .5 kg
⅓ cup sliced green onions   80 ml

- Drain peaches, reserve ½ cup (120 ml) juice in large skillet and set peaches aside.

- Add brown sugar and mustard to skillet, bring to a boil over medium-high heat and cook 2 minutes or until slightly reduced.

- Add ham and cook 2 minutes on each side.

- Add peaches and green onions, cover and cook over low heat for 3 minutes or until peaches are thoroughly hot.

Baked Ham and Pineapple

1 (6 - 8 pound) fully cooked, bone-in ham	2.7 kg
Whole cloves	
½ cup packed brown sugar	120 ml
1 (8 ounce) can sliced pineapple with juice	227 g
5 maraschino cherries	

- Preheat oven to 325° (162° C).

- Place ham in roasting pan, score surface with shallow diagonal cuts making diamond shapes and insert cloves into diamonds.

- Cover and bake for 1 hour 30 minutes.

- Combine brown sugar and juice from pineapple and pour over ham.

- Arrange pineapple slices and cherries on ham. Bake uncovered, additional 40 minutes.

Praline Ham

2 (½ inch) thick ham slices, cooked (about 2½ pounds)	2 (1.2 cm)/1.2 kg
½ cup maple syrup	120 ml
3 tablespoons brown sugar	45 ml
1 tablespoon butter	15 ml
⅓ cup chopped pecans	80 ml

- Heat ham slices in shallow pan at 325° (162° C) for 10 minutes.

- Bring syrup, sugar and butter to a boil in small saucepan and stir often. Stir in pecans and spoon syrup mixture over ham. Warm additional 20 minutes.

Sausage Casserole

1 pound pork sausage	.5 kg
2 (15 ounce) cans pork and beans	2 (425 g)
1 (15 ounce) can Mexican stewed tomatoes	425 g
1 (8 ounce) package cornbread muffin mix	227 g

- Preheat oven to 400° (204° C).

- Brown sausage and drain fat. Add beans and tomatoes, blend and bring to a boil. Pour mixture into sprayed 3-quart (3 L) baking dish.

- Prepare muffin mix according to package directions and drop by teaspoonfuls over meat-bean mixture. Bake for 30 minutes or until top browns.

Apricot-Baked Ham

1 (12 - 20 pound) whole ham, fully cooked	
Whole cloves	
2 tablespoons dry mustard	30 ml
1¼ cups apricot jam	300 ml
1¼ cups packed light brown sugar	300 ml

- Preheat oven to 450° (230° C).

- Place ham on rack in large roasting pan and insert cloves into ham every inch or so.

- Combine dry mustard and jam and spread over entire surface of ham.

- Pat brown sugar over jam mixture. Reduce heat to 325° (162° C) and bake uncovered for 15 minutes per pound.

The best way to avoid freezer burn is to wrap food twice in plastic wrap and seal in an air-tight plastic bag. Be sure to date your package and label it with a permanent marker.

Walnut-Ham Linguine

2 teaspoons minced garlic	10 ml
½ cup coarsely chopped walnuts	120 ml
1 sweet red bell pepper, thinly slice	
¼ cup olive oil	60 ml
½ pound cooked ham, cut in strips	227 g
1 (16 ounce) jar creamy alfredo sauce	.5 kg
¼ cup grated parmesan cheese	60 ml
1 (12 ounce) package linguine, cooked al dente	340 g
1 cup seasoned breadcrumbs	240 ml

- Preheat oven to 350° (176° C).

- In large skillet, saute garlic, walnuts and bell pepper in oil for 1 to 2 minutes.

- In large bowl, combine garlic-bell pepper mixture, ham, alfredo sauce, parmesan cheese and linguine and mix well.

- Spoon into sprayed 3-quart (3 L) baking dish. Sprinkle breadcrumbs over top.

- Bake uncovered for 35 minutes or until breadcrumbs are light brown.

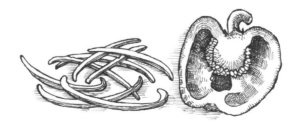

Sandwich Souffle

A fun lunch!

Butter, softened
8 slices white bread, crusts removed
4 slices ham
4 slices American cheese
2 cups milk   480 ml
2 eggs, beaten

- Preheat oven to 375° (190° C).

- Butter bread on both sides, make 4 sandwiches with ham and cheese.

- Place sandwiches in sprayed 8-inch (20 cm) square baking pan. Beat milk, eggs and a little salt and pepper. Pour over sandwiches and soak for 1 to 2 hours.   Bake for 45 to 50 minutes.

Grilled Pork Loin

1 (4 pound) boneless pork loin roast	1.8 kg
1 (8 ounce) bottle Italian salad dressing	227 g
1 cup dry white wine	240 ml
3 cloves garlic, minced	
10 black peppercorns	

- Pierce roast at 1-inch (2.5 cm) intervals with fork and set aside.

- Combine salad dressing, white wine, garlic and peppercorns. Reserve ½ cup (120 ml) mixture for basting during grilling.

- Place roast in large, resealable plastic bag with remaining mixture, chill 8 hours and turn occasionally.

- Remove roast from marinade and discard marinade.

- Place roast on rack in grill.

- Cook, covered with grill lid, for 35 minutes or until meat thermometer inserted into thickest portion reaches 160° (71° C). Turn occasionally and baste with ½ cup (120 ml) reserved dressing mixture.

Ham and Potatoes Olé!

1 (24 ounce) package frozen hash browns with onion and peppers, thawed	680 g
3 cups cubed, cooked ham	710 ml
1 (10 ounce) can cream of chicken soup	280 g
1 (10 ounce) can fiesta nacho cheese soup	280 g
1 cup hot salsa	240 ml
1 (8 ounce) package shredded cheddar-Jack cheese	227 g

- Preheat oven to 350° (176° C). Combine potatoes, ham, both soups and salsa in large bowl and mix well.

- Spoon into sprayed 9 x 13-inch (23 x 33 cm) baking dish. Cover and cook for 40 minutes. Remove from oven, sprinkle cheese over casserole and bake uncovered additional 5 minutes.

Pineapple Sauce for Ham

Pre-sliced, cooked honey-baked ham slices	
1 (15 ounce) can pineapple chunks with juice	425 g
1 cup apricot preserves	240 ml
1¼ cups packed brown sugar	300 ml
¼ teaspoon cinnamon	1 ml

- Place ham slices in shallow baking pan. In saucepan, combine pineapple preserves, brown sugar and cinnamon and heat.

- Pour sauce over ham slices and heat.

Lemonade Spareribs

4 pounds pork spareribs	1.8 kg
1 (6 ounce) can lemonade concentrate	168 g
½ teaspoon garlic salt	2 ml
⅓ cup soy sauce	80 ml

- Preheat oven to 350° (176° C).

- Place ribs, meaty-side down, in shallow roasting pan and cook covered for 40 minutes.

- Remove cover, drain fat and return ribs to oven.

- Bake additional 30 minutes and drain fat again.

- Combine lemonade concentrate, garlic salt and soy sauce and brush on ribs.

- Reduce temperature to 325° (162° C), cover and bake for additional 1 hour or until ribs are tender. Brush occasionally with sauce.

Tequila Baby-Back Ribs

4 pounds baby-back pork ribs	1.8 kg
1 (12 ounce) bottle tequila-lime marinade, divided	340 g

- Cut ribs in lengths to fit in large, sealable plastic bag.

- Place ribs add ¾ cup (180 ml) marinade and a little pepper in bag and shake to coat. Refrigerate overnight. Place ribs in sprayed shallow baking dish and discard used marinade.

- Cover ribs with foil and bake at 375° (190° C) for 30 minutes. Remove from oven and spread remaining marinade over ribs.

- Reduce heat to 300° (148° C) and cook 1 hour. Uncover to let ribs brown and bake additional 30 minutes.

Hawaiian Aloha Pork

This is great served over rice.

1 (2 pound) lean pork tenderloin, cut into 1-inch cubes	1 kg/2.5 cm
1 (15 ounce) can pineapple chunks with juice	425 g
1 (12 ounce) bottle chili sauce	340 g
1 teaspoon ground ginger	5 ml

- In skillet, season pork with a little salt and pepper. Combine meat, pineapple with juice, chili sauce and ginger. Simmer covered for 1 hour 30 minutes.

Sweet-and-Sour Spareribs

3 - 4 pounds spareribs	
3 tablespoons soy sauce	45 ml
⅓ cup mustard	80 ml
1 cup packed brown sugar	240 ml
½ teaspoon garlic salt	2 ml

- Place spareribs in roasting pan, bake at 325° (162° C) for 45 minutes and drain.

- Make sauce with soy sauce, mustard, brown sugar and garlic salt and brush on ribs.

- Return to oven, reduce heat to 300° (148° C) and bake for 2 hours or until ribs are tender. Baste several times.

Tenderloin with Apricot Sauce

3 pounds pork tenderloins	1.3 kg
1 cup apricot preserves	240 ml
⅓ cup lemon juice	80 ml
⅓ cup ketchup	80 ml
1 tablespoon soy sauce	15 ml

- Preheat oven to 325° (162° C). Place tenderloins in roasting pan. Combine preserves, lemon juice, ketchup and soy sauce.

- Pour preserve mixture over pork and bake covered for 1 hour 20 minutes. Baste once. Serve over rice.

One-Dish Pork and Peas

So many of our casseroles are chicken, but pork is so good and always tender. This blend of ingredients makes a delicious dish.

2 pounds pork tenderloin	1 kg
2 tablespoons oil, divided	30 ml
1½ cups celery, sliced	360 ml
1 large onion, chopped	
2 sweet red bell peppers, seeded, chopped	
1 (12 ounce) package small egg noodles, cooked, drained	340 g
1 (10 ounce) can cream of chicken soup	280 g
1 (10 ounce) can chicken broth	280 g
1 (8 ounce) carton whipping cream	227 g
1 (10 ounce) package frozen green peas, thawed	280 g
1½ teaspoons seasoned salt	7 ml
1 teaspoon black pepper	5 ml
1½ cups seasoned dry breadcrumbs	360 ml
¾ cup chopped walnuts	180 ml

- Preheat oven to 350° (176° C).

- Cut pork tenderloin into ½-inch cubes. In large skillet, brown pork in 1 tablespoon (15 ml) oil. Reduce heat and cook 25 minutes. Remove pork to separate dish. In a little oil, saute celery, onion and bell pepper.

- Add pork, noodles, soup, broth, whipping cream, peas, 1 ½ teaspoons (7 ml) salt and 1 teaspoon (5 ml) pepper; mix well. Spoon into sprayed 10 x 15-inch (25 x 38 cm) baking dish. Sprinkle with breadcrumbs and walnuts.

- Bake uncovered for 35 to 45 minutes or until bubbly around edges and breadcrumbs are light brown. Serves 20.

SEAFOOD

Crispy Fish and Cheese Filets

2 pounds fish fillets	1 kg
½ cup prepared creamy ranch-style salad dressing	120 ml
1½ cups crushed cheese crackers	360 ml
2 tablespoons butter, melted	30 ml

- Preheat oven to 425° (220° C).

- Cut fish into serving portions, dip into dressing and roll in cracker crumbs.

- Place in sprayed shallow pan and drizzle butter over fish.

- Bake uncovered for 15 minutes or until fish flakes easily.

There is usually a thin end on most fish fillets. When cooking fillets, wrap thin end over fillet until it is about the same thickness as the thicker end.

Baked Fish

1 pound fish filets	.5 kg
3 tablespoons butter	45 ml
1 teaspoon tarragon	5 ml
2 teaspoons capers	10 ml
2 tablespoons lemon juice	30 ml

- Preheat oven to 375° (190° C).

- Place fish filets and a little butter in sprayed shallow pan and sprinkle with a little salt and pepper.

- Bake for about 5 to 16 minutes, turn and bake additional 4 to 6 minutes or until fish flakes.

- For sauce, melt 3 tablespoons (45 ml) butter with tarragon, capers and lemon juice and serve over warm fish.

Chips and Fish

3 - 4 fish filets, rinsed, dried
1 cup mayonnaise   240 ml
2 tablespoons fresh lime juice and lime wedges   30 ml
1½ cups crushed corn chips   360 ml

- Preheat oven to 425Υ (220° C).

- Mix mayonnaise and lime juice and spread on both sides of fish filets.

- Place crushed corn chips on wax paper, dredge both sides of fish in chips and shake off excess chips.

- Place filets on foil-covered baking sheet and bake for 15 minutes or until fish flakes.

- Serve with lime wedges.

Tilapia is a great, inexpensive fish that can be baked, pan-fried or used in the recipe above.

Golden Catfish Filets

3 eggs	
¾ cup flour	180 ml
¾ cup cornmeal	180 ml
1 teaspoon garlic powder	5 ml
6 - 8 (4 - 8 ounce) catfish filets	6 - 8 (114 g)

- In shallow bowl, beat eggs until foamy.

- In another shallow bowl, combine flour, cornmeal, garlic powder and a little salt.

- Dip filets in eggs and coat with cornmeal mixture.

- Heat ¼-inch (.6 cm) oil in large skillet and fry fish over medium-high heat for about 4 minutes on each side or until fish flakes easily with fork.

Fish like salmon, tuna and mackerel are considered fatty fish, but are still thought of as healthy and nutritional. It is thought that fish help to prevent heart disease and even aid in preventing diseases like Alzheimer's and strokes.

Flounder au Gratin

½ cup fine dry breadcrumbs	120 ml
¼ cup grated parmesan cheese	60 ml
1 pound flounder filets	.5 kg
⅓ cup mayonnaise	80 ml

- Preheat oven to 375° (190° C).

- In shallow dish, combine crumbs and cheese.

- Brush both sides of fish with mayonnaise and coat with crumb mixture.

- Arrange filets in single layer in shallow pan and bake for 20 to 25 minutes or until fish flakes easily.

Flounder filets will usually have the skin in tact
In this case, look for skin with a glossy appearance.
If the fish is whole, make sure the eye is clear, not foggy.

Lemon-Dill Filets

½ cup mayonnaise	120 ml
2 tablespoons lemon juice	30 ml
½ teaspoon lemon zest	2 ml
1 teaspoon dill weed	5 ml
1 pound cod or flounder filets	.5 kg

- Combine mayonnaise, lemon juice, lemon zest and dill weed until they blend well.

- Place fish on sprayed grill or broiler rack and brush with half mayonnaise mixture.

- Grill or broil 5 to 8 minutes, turn and brush with remaining mayonnaise mixture.

- Continue grilling or broiling 5 to 8 minutes or until fish flakes easily with fork.

Lemon-Baked Fish

1 pound sole or halibut filets	.5 kg
2 tablespoons butter	30 ml
1 teaspoon dried tarragon	5 ml
2 tablespoons lemon juice	30 ml

- Preheat oven to 375° (190° C).

- Place fish filets in sprayed shallow pan with a little butter and sprinkle with a little salt and pepper.

- Bake for 8 to 10 minutes, turn and bake additional 6 minutes or until fish flakes.

- Melt 2 tablespoons (30 ml) butter with tarragon and lemon juice and serve over warm fish filets.

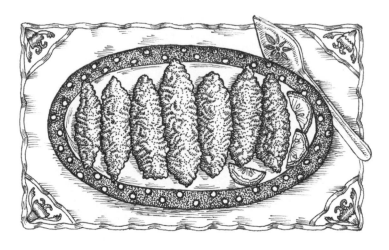

Baked Halibut

2 (1 inch) thick halibut steaks	2 (2.5 cm)
1 (8 ounce) carton sour cream	227 g
½ cup grated parmesan cheese	120 ml
¾ teaspoon dill weed	4 ml

- Preheat oven to 325° (162° C).

- Place halibut in sprayed 9 x 13-inch (23 x 33 cm) baking dish.

- Combine sour cream, parmesan cheese and dill weed (and salt and pepper, if desired) and spoon over halibut.

- Cover and bake for 20 minutes.

- Uncover and sprinkle with paprika.

- Bake additional 10 minutes or until fish flakes easily with fork.

The halibut is a relative of the flounder, albeit a much, much larger one. Halibut are found in cold waters and can weigh as much as 600 pounds.

Orange Roughy with Peppers

1 pound orange roughy filets   .5 kg
1 onion, sliced
2 red bell peppers, cut into julienne strips
1 teaspoon dried thyme leaves   5 ml

- Cut fish into 4 serving-size pieces.

- Heat a little oil in skillet, layer onion and bell peppers in oil and sprinkle with half thyme and ¼ teaspoon pepper.

- Place fish over peppers and sprinkle with remaining thyme.

- Turn burner on high just until fish begins to cook.

- Lower heat, cover and cook fish for 15 to 20 minutes or until fish flakes easily.

*When buying a whole fish check to make sure the eyes are clear
and the meat is firm.
When buying fillets or steaks, be sure meat is uniform in
color with no brown spots.*

Chipper Fish

2 pounds sole or orange roughy	1 kg
½ cup Caesar salad dressing	120 ml
1 cup crushed potato chips	240 ml
½ cup shredded cheddar cheese	120 ml

- Preheat oven to 375° (190° C).

- Dip fish in dressing and place in sprayed baking dish.

- Combine potato chips and cheese and sprinkle over fish.

- Bake for about 20 to 25 minutes.

The most important thing to remember about cooking fish is not to overcook it. The internal temperature should be about 145° and the meat should be opaque. Don't let fish dry out.

Boiled Shrimp

3 pounds fresh shrimp	1.3 kg
2 teaspoons seafood seasoning	10 ml
½ cup vinegar	120 ml

- Remove heads from shrimp.
- Place all ingredients and 1 teaspoon (5 ml) salt in large saucepan, cover shrimp with water and bring to a boil.
- Reduce heat and boil for 10 minutes.
- Remove from heat, drain and chill.

Beer-Batter Shrimp

1 (12 ounce) can beer	340 g
1 cup flour	240 ml
2 teaspoons garlic powder	10 ml
1 pound shrimp, peeled, veined	.5kg

- Combine beer, flour and garlic powder and stir to creamy consistency to make batter.
- Dip shrimp into batter to cover and deep fry in hot oil.

Seafood Delight

1 (6 ounce) can shrimp, drained	168 g
1 (6 ounce) can crabmeat, drained, flaked	168 g
1 (10 ounce) can corn or potato chowder	280 g
2 - 3 cups dry, seasoned breadcrumbs, divided	480 ml

- Preheat oven to 350° (176° C).

- Mix shrimp, crabmeat, chowder and ⅓ cup (80 ml) breadcrumbs.

- Place mixture in sprayed 1½-quart (1.5 L) baking dish and sprinkle with remaining breadcrumbs.

- Bake for 30 minutes or until casserole bubbles and breadcrumbs are light brown.

Creamed Shrimp Over Rice

3 (10 ounce) cans frozen cream of shrimp soup	3 (280 g)
1 (1 pint) carton sour cream	.5 kg
1½ teaspoons curry powder	7 ml
2 (5 ounce) cans veined shrimp	2 (143 g)

- Combine all ingredients in double boiler.

- Heat and stir constantly, but do not boil.

- Serve over hot, cooked rice.

Crabmeat Casserole

2 (6 ounce) cans crabmeat, drained, flaked	2 (168 g)
1 (3 ounce) can french-fried onions, divided	84 g
1 (10 ounce) can cream of chicken soup	280 g
¾ cup cracker crumbs	180 ml

- Preheat oven to 350° (176° C).

- In bowl, combine crabmeat, half fried onions, soup and cracker crumbs and mix well.

- Place in sprayed baking dish and top with remaining onions. Bake covered for 30 minutes.

Tuna and Chips

1 (6 ounce) can tuna, drained	168 g
1 (10 ounce) can cream of chicken soup	280 g
¾ cup milk	180 ml
1½ cups crushed potato chips, divided	360 ml

- Preheat oven to 350° (176° C).

- Break chunks of tuna into bowl and stir in soup and milk. Add ¾ cup (180 ml) crushed potato chips and mix well.

- Pour mixture into sprayed baking dish and sprinkle remaining chips over top.

- Bake uncovered for 30 minutes or until chips are light brown.

Crab Mornay

2 (6 ounce) cans crabmeat, drained	2 (168 g)
1 cup cream of mushroom soup	240 ml
½ cup shredded Swiss cheese	120 ml
½ cup seasoned breadcrumbs	120 ml

- Preheat oven to 350° (176° C).

- Combine crabmeat, soup and cheese and mix well.

- Pour into sprayed 1½-quart (1.5 L) baking dish and sprinkle with breadcrumbs.

- Bake uncovered for 30 minutes or until soup bubbles and breadcrumbs are brown.

Baked Oysters

1 cup oysters, drained, rinsed	240 ml
2 cups cracker crumbs	480 ml
¼ cup (½ stick) butter, melted	60 ml
½ cup milk	120 ml

- Preheat oven to 350° (176° C).

- Make alternating layers of oysters, cracker crumbs and butter in 7 x 11-inch (18 x 28 cm) baking dish.

- Pour warmed milk over layers and add lots of salt and pepper.

- Bake for 35 minutes.

Salmon Croquets

1 (15 ounce) can pink salmon, drained, flaked   425 g
1 egg
½ cup biscuit mix   120 ml
¼ cup ketchup   60 ml

- Combine salmon (discard skin and bones) and egg in bowl.

- Add biscuit mix and ketchup and mix well. Shape croquet into triangle-shaped legs about 3 inches (8 cm) long.

- Heat a little oil in skillet and place each croquet into skillet.

- Cook each side until brown.

Before squeezing the juice from lemons, limes or oranges, scrape the outside rind (called zest) to get just the colored part of the rind. Even if your recipe doesn't call for it, save it in air-tight plastic bags for flavoring all kinds of dishes.

DESSERTS

Pecan-Topped Toffee

1 cup (2 sticks) butter	240 ml
1¼ cups packed brown sugar	300 ml
6 (1.5 ounce) milk chocolate bars	6 (45 g)
⅔ cup finely chopped pecans	160 ml

- In saucepan, combine butter and brown sugar and cook on medium-high heat.

- Stir constantly until mixture reaches 300° (148° C) on candy thermometer and pour immediately into sprayed 9-inch (23 cm) baking pan.

- Lay chocolate bars evenly over hot candy.

- When chocolate is soft, spread into smooth layer.

- Sprinkle pecans over chocolate and press lightly with back of spoon.

- Chill in refrigerator for 1 hour.

- Invert candy onto wax paper and break into small, irregular pieces.

Microwave Pralines

1½ cups packed brown sugar	360 ml
⅔ cup half-and-half cream	160 ml
2 tablespoons butter, melted	30 ml
1⅔ cups chopped pecans	400 ml

- Combine brown sugar, half-and-half and dash of salt in deep glass dish and mix well. Blend in butter.

- Microwave on HIGH for 10 minutes, stir once and add pecans. Cool for 1 minute.

- Beat by hand until creamy and thick, about 4 to 5 minutes. (The mixture will lose some of its gloss.)

- Drop by tablespoonfuls onto wax paper.

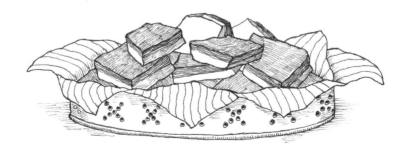

Dream Candy

2 (8 ounce) cartons whipping cream	2 (227 g)
3 cups sugar	710 ml
1 cup light corn syrup	240 ml
1 cup chopped pecans	240 ml

- In saucepan, combine whipping cream, sugar and corn syrup and cook to soft-ball stage (234Y/115° C on candy thermometer).

- Stir and beat until candy is cool. Add pecans and pour into sprayed 9-inch (23 cm) pan.

Caramel Crunch

½ cup firmly packed brown sugar	120 ml
½ cup light corn syrup	120 ml
4 tablespoons (½ stick) butter	60 ml
6 cups bite-size crispy corn cereal squares	1.5 L
2 cups peanuts	480 ml

- In large saucepan, heat brown sugar, syrup and butter. Stir constantly until sugar and butter melt.

- Add cereal and peanuts and stir until all ingredients are well coated.

- Spread mixture on lightly sprayed baking sheet and bake at 250Y (121° C) for 30 minutes. Stir occasionally while baking.

- Cool and store in airtight container.

Peanut Brittle

2 cups sugar	480 ml
½ cup light corn syrup	120 ml
2 cups dry-roasted peanuts	480 ml
1 tablespoon butter	15 ml
1 teaspoon baking soda	5 ml

- Combine sugar and corn syrup in saucepan. Stir constantly over low heat until sugar dissolves. Cover and cook over medium heat another 2 minutes.

- Uncover, add peanuts and cook, stirring occasionally, to hard-crack stage 300° (148° C). Stir in butter and baking soda, pour into sprayed jellyroll pan and spread thinly. Cool and break into pieces.

White Chocolate Fudge

This is a little different slant to fudge; really creamy and really good!

1 (8 ounce) package cream cheese, softened	227 g
4 cups powdered sugar	1 L
1½ teaspoons vanilla extract	7 ml
1 (12 ounce) package almond bark, melted	340 g
¾ cup chopped pecans	180 ml

- Beat cream cheese at medium speed with mixer until smooth, gradually add powdered sugar and vanilla and beat well. Stir in melted almond bark and pecans and spread into sprayed 8-inch (20 cm) square pan.

- Refrigerate until firm and cut into small squares.

Diamond Fudge

1 (6 ounce) package semi-sweet chocolate chips	168 g
1 cup creamy peanut butter	240 ml
½ cup (1 stick) butter	120 ml
1 cup powdered sugar	240 ml

- Combine chips, peanut butter and butter in saucepan over low heat. Stir constantly, just until mixture melts and is smooth.

- Remove from heat, add powdered sugar and stir until smooth.

- Spoon into sprayed 8-inch (20 cm) square pan and chill until firm.

- Let stand 10 minutes at room temperature before cutting into squares and store in refrigerator.

Microwave Fudge

3 cups semi-sweet chocolate chips	710 m
1 (14 ounce) can sweetened condensed milk	396 g
¼ cup (½ stick) butter, sliced	60 ml
1 cup chopped walnuts	240 ml

- Combine chocolate chips, sweetened condensed milk and butter in 2-quart (2 L) glass bowl.
- Microwave on MEDIUM for 4 to 5 minutes and stir at 1½-minute intervals.
- Stir in walnuts and pour into sprayed 8-inch (20 cm) square dish.
- Chill 2 hours and cut into squares.

Nutty Blonde Brownies

1 (16 ounce) box light brown sugar	.5 kg
4 eggs	
2 cups biscuit mix	480 ml
2 cups chopped pecans	480 ml

- Preheat oven to 350° (176° C).
- In mixing bowl, beat brown sugar, eggs and biscuit mix.
- Stir in pecans and pour into sprayed 9 x 13-inch (23 x 33 cm) baking pan.
- Bake for 35 minutes, cool and cut into squares.

Snicker Brownies

1 (18 ounce) box German chocolate cake mix	510 g
¾ cup (1½ sticks) butter, melted	180 ml
½ cup evaporated milk	120 ml
4 (2.7 ounce) Snicker® candy bars,	
cut in ⅛-inch slices	4 (70 g)

- Preheat oven to 350° (176° C).

- In large bowl, combine cake mix, butter and evaporated milk and beat on low speed until mixture blends well.

- Place half batter in sprayed, floured 9 x 13-inch (23 x 33 cm) baking pan and bake for 10 minutes.

- Remove from oven and place candy bar slices evenly over brownies.

- Drop remaining half of batter by spoonfuls over candy bars and spread as evenly as possible.

- Return to oven and bake for additional 20 minutes. When cool, cut into bars.

Brownies are really easy to make and always a popular choice. About the only way you can really mess up brownies is to overcook them. Fudgy brownies are a little better if they are slightly undercooked. Cake brownies are best with icing.

Gooey Turtle Bars

½ cup (1 stick) butter, melted	120 ml
2 cups vanilla wafer crumbs	480 ml
1 (12 ounce) semi-sweet chocolate chips	340 g
1 cup pecan pieces	240 ml
1 (12 ounce) jar caramel topping	340 g

- Preheat oven to 350° (176° C).

- Combine butter and wafer crumbs in 9 x 13-inch (23 x 33 cm) baking pan and press into bottom of pan. Sprinkle with chocolate chips and pecans.

- Remove lid from caramel topping and microwave on HIGH for 30 seconds or until hot. Drizzle topping over pecans.

- Bake for about 15 minutes or until chocolate chips melt. (Make sure chocolate melts but crumbs don't burn.)

- Cool in pan and chill at least 30 minutes before cutting into squares.

TIP: Watch bars closely—you want the chips to melt, but you don't want the crumbs to burn.

Apricot Bars

1¼ cups flour	300 ml
¾ cup packed brown sugar	180 ml
6 tablespoons (¾ stick) butter	90 ml
¾ cup apricot preserves	180 ml

- Preheat oven to 350° (176° C).

- In mixing bowl, combine flour, brown sugar and butter and mix well.

- Place half mixture in 9-inch (23 cm) square baking pan, spread apricot preserves over top and sprinkle with remaining flour mixture. Bake for 30 minutes. Cut into squares.

Walnut Bars

1⅔ cups graham cracker crumbs	400 ml
1½ cups coarsely chopped walnuts	360 ml
1 (14 ounce) can sweetened condensed milk	396 g
¼ cup flaked coconut, optional	60 ml

- Preheat oven to 350° (176° C). Place graham cracker crumbs and walnuts in bowl.

- Slowly add sweetened condensed milk, coconut and a dash of salt. (Mixture will be very thick.) Pack into sprayed 9-inch (23 cm) square pan and press mixture down with back of spoon.

- Bake for 35 minutes and cut into squares when cool.

Pecan Squares

1 (24 ounce) package white almond bark	680 g
1 cup cinnamon chips	240 ml
1 cup chopped pecans	240 ml
8 cups frosted rice crispy cereal	1.8 L

- Melt almond bark and cinnamon chips in very large saucepan or roasting pan on low heat and stir constantly until they melt.

- Remove from heat and add pecans and cereal. Mix well and stir into 9 x 13-inch (23 x 33 cm) pan. Pat down with back of spoon, refrigerate just until set and cut into squares.

Chinese Cookies

1 (6 ounce) package butterscotch chips	168 g
1 (6 ounce) package chocolate chips	168 g
2 cups chow mein noodles	480 ml
1¼ cups salted peanuts	300 ml

- On low heat, melt butterscotch and chocolate chips. Add noodles and peanuts and mix well.

- Drop by teaspoonfuls onto wax paper and refrigerate to harden.

- Store in airtight container.

Butterscotch Cookies

1 (12 ounce) and 1 (6 ounce) package butterscotch chips	340 g
2¼ cups chow mein noodles	540 ml
½ cup chopped walnuts	120 ml
¼ cup flaked coconut	60 ml

- Melt butterscotch chips in double boiler. Add noodles, walnuts and coconut.

- Drop by tablespoonfuls onto wax paper.

Coconut Yummies

1 (12 ounce) package white chocolate
   baking chips   340 g
¼ cup (½ stick) butter   60 ml
16 large marshmallows
2 cups quick-cooking oats   480 ml
1 cup flaked coconut   240 ml

- In saucepan over low heat, melt chocolate chips, butter and marshmallows and stir until smooth.
- Stir in oats and coconut and mix well.
- Drop by rounded teaspoonfuls onto wax paper-lined baking sheets.
- Chill until set and store in airtight container.

Haystacks

1 (12 ounce) package butterscotch chips   340 g
1 cup salted peanuts   240 ml
1½ cups chow mein noodles   360 ml

- Melt butterscotch chips in top of double boiler.
- Remove from heat and stir in peanuts and noodles.
- Drop by teaspoonfuls onto wax paper.
- Cool and store in airtight container.

Orange Balls

1 (12 ounce) box vanilla wafers, crushed	340 g
½ cup (1 stick) butter, melted	120 ml
1 (16 ounce) box powdered sugar	.5 kg
1 (6 ounce) can frozen orange juice concentrate	168 g
1 cup finely chopped pecans	240 ml

- Combine wafer crumbs, butter, sugar and orange juice concentrate and mix well.

- Form into balls, roll in chopped pecans and store in airtight container.

- Make these in finger shapes for something different. They make neat cookies for a party or a tea.

Peanut Butter Crunchies

1 cup sugar	240 ml
½ cup white corn syrup	120 ml
2 cups peanut butter	480 ml
4 cups rice crispy cereal	1 L

- In saucepan, mix sugar and syrup and bring to a rolling boil.

- Remove from stove and stir in peanut butter. Add cereal and mix well.

- Drop by teaspoonfuls onto wax paper and place in refrigerator for a few minutes to set.

Scotch Shortbread

½ cup (1 stick) unsalted butter, softened	120 ml
⅓ cup sugar	80 ml
1¼ cups flour	300 ml
Powdered sugar	

- Preheat oven to 325° (162° C).

- Cream butter and sugar until light and fluffy. Add flour and a dash of salt and mix well.

- Spread dough into 8-inch (20 cm) square pan and bake for 20 minutes or until light brown. Let shortbread cool in pan, dust with powdered sugar and cut into squares.

Sand Tarts

1 cup (2 sticks) butter, softened	240 ml
¾ cup powdered sugar	180 ml
2 cups sifted flour	480 ml
1 cup chopped pecans	240 ml
1 teaspoon vanilla extract	5 ml

- Preheat oven to 325° (162° C).

- With mixer, cream butter and powdered sugar and add flour, pecans and vanilla.

- Roll into crescents and place on unsprayed baking sheet. Bake for 20 minutes and roll in extra powdered sugar after tarts cool.

Pecan Puffs

2 egg whites	
¾ cup packed light brown sugar	180 ml
1 teaspoon vanilla extract	5 ml
1 cup chopped pecans	240 ml

- Preheat oven to 250° (121° C).

- Beat egg whites until foamy and add brown sugar ¼ cup (60 ml) at a time.

- Add vanilla, continue beating until stiff peaks form (about 3 or 4 minutes) and fold in pecans.

- Line baking sheet with freezer paper and drop mixture by teaspoonfuls onto paper.

- Bake for 45 minutes.

Coconut Macaroons

2 (7 ounce) packages flaked coconut	2 (198 g)
1 (14 ounce) can sweetened condensed milk	396 g
2 teaspoons vanilla extract	10 ml
½ teaspoon almond extract	2 ml

- Preheat oven to 350° (176° C). In mixing bowl, combine coconut, sweetened condensed milk and extracts and mix well.

- Drop by rounded teaspoonfuls onto foil-lined baking sheet. Bake for 8 to 10 minutes or until light brown around edges.

- Immediately remove from foil. (Macaroons will stick if allowed to cool.) Store at room temperature.

Butter Cookies

1 pound butter	.5 kg
¾ cup packed brown sugar	180 ml
¾ cup granulated sugar	180 ml
4½ cups flour	1.1 L

- Preheat oven to 350° (176° C). Cream butter and sugars, slowly add flour and mix well. (Batter will be very thick.)

- Roll into small balls and place on unsprayed baking sheet. Bake for about 15 minutes until only slightly brown. (Do not overbake.)

Devil's Food Cookies

1 (18 ounce) box devil's food cake mix	510 g
½ cup oil	120 ml
2 eggs	
¾ cup chopped pecans, optional	180 ml

- Preheat oven to 350° (176° C).

- Combine cake mix, oil and eggs in bowl and mix well. (If you like, fold in chopped pecans.)

- Drop by teaspoonfuls onto non-stick baking sheet.

- Bake for 10 to 12 minutes. Cool and remove to wire rack.

Brown Sugar Cookies

¾ cup packed brown sugar	180 ml
1 cup (2 sticks) butter, softened	240 ml
1 egg yolk	
2 cups flour	480 ml

- Cream sugar and butter until light and fluffy.

- Mix in egg yolk and blend in flour. Refrigerate dough for 1 hour.

- Form dough into 1-inch (2.5 cm) balls, flatten and criss-cross with fork on lightly sprayed baking sheet.

- Bake at 325° (162° C) for 10 to 12 minutes or until golden brown.

Cherry Crisp

2 (20 ounce) cans cherry pie filling 2 (567 g)
1 (18 ounce) box white cake mix 510 g
½ cup (1 stick) butter 120 ml
2 cups chopped pecans 480 ml

- Preheat oven to 350° (176° C).

- Pour pie filling into sprayed 9 x 13-inch (23 x 33 cm) baking dish. Sprinkle cake mix over top of filling.

- Dot with butter and cover with pecans. Bake uncovered for 45 minutes.

Blueberry Crunch

1 (20 ounce) can crushed pineapple with juice 567 g
1 (18 ounce) box yellow cake mix 510 g
3 cups fresh or frozen blueberries 710 m
⅔ cup sugar 160 ml
½ cup (1 stick) butter, melted 120 ml

- Preheat oven to 350° (176° C).

- Spread pineapple in sprayed 9 x 13-inch (23 x 33 cm) baking dish and sprinkle cake mix, blueberries and sugar.

- Drizzle with butter and bake for 45 minutes or until bubbly.

Apricot Cobbler

So easy and so good!

1 (20 ounce) can apricot pie filling	567 g
1 (20 ounce) can crushed pineapple with juice	567 g
1 cup chopped pecans	240 ml
1 (18 ounce) box yellow cake mix	510 g
1 cup (2 sticks) butter, melted	240 ml

- Preheat oven to 375° (190° C).

- Spray 9 x 13-inch (23 x 33 cm) baking. Pour pie filling in pan and spread.

- Spoon pineapple and juice over pie filling and sprinkle pecans over pineapple.

- Sprinkle cake mix over pecans.

- Drizzle melted butter over cake mix and bake for 40 minutes or until light brown and crunchy.

- Serve hot or room temperature. (It's great topped with whipped topping.)

Cherry Cobbler

2 (20 ounce) cans cherry pie filling	2 (567 g)
1 (18 ounce) box white cake mix	510 g
¾ cup (1½ sticks) butter, melted	180 ml
1 (4 ounce) package almonds, slivered	114 g

- Preheat oven to 350° (176° C).

- Spread pie filling in sprayed 9 x 13-inch (23 x 33 cm) baking pan. Sprinkle cake mix over pie filling, drizzle with melted butter and sprinkle almonds over top.

- Bake for 45 minutes. Top with whipped topping.

Easy Pumpkin Pie

2 eggs	
1 (30 ounce) can pumpkin pie mix	810 g
1 (5 ounce) can evaporated milk	143 g
1 (9 inch) deep-dish piecrust	23 cm

- Preheat oven to 400° (204° C).

- Beat eggs lightly in large bowl and stir in pumpkin pie mix and evaporated milk. Pour into piecrust. (Cover piecrust edges with strips of foil to prevent excessive browning.)

- Bake for 15 minutes. Reduce temperature to 325Υ (162° C) and bake for additional 40 minutes or until knife inserted in center comes out clean and cool.

Black Forest Pie

This is definitely a party dessert, but the family will insist it should be served on a regular basis.

4 (1 ounce) squares unsweetened baking chocolate	4 (28 g)
1 (14 ounce) can sweetened condensed milk	396 g
1 teaspoon almond extract	5 ml
1½ cups whipping cream, whipped	360 ml
1 (9 inch) prepared piecrust	23 cm
1 (20 ounce) can cherry pie filling, chilled	567 g

- In saucepan over medium-low heat, melt chocolate with sweetened condensed milk and stir well to mix.

- Remove from heat and stir in extract. (This mixture needs to cool.)

- When mixture is about room temperature, pour chocolate into whipped cream and fold gently until they combine.

- Pour into piecrust.

- To serve, spoon heaping spoonful of cherry filling over each piece of pie.

*Do not keep chocolate in the refrigerator.
It is best stored between 60° and 70°.*

Easy Chocolate Pie

1 (8 ounce) milk chocolate candy bar	227 g
1 (16 ounce) carton frozen whipped topping, thawed, divided	.5 kg
¾ cup chopped pecans	180 ml
1 (9 inch) prepared piecrust	23 cm

- In saucepan, break candy into small pieces and melt over low heat. Remove and cool several minutes.

- Fold in two-thirds whipped topping, mix well and stir in chopped pecans. Pour into piecrust, spread remaining whipped topping over top and chill for at least 8 hours.

Dixie Pie

24 large marshmallows	
1 cup evaporated milk	240 ml
1 (8 ounce) carton whipping cream, whipped	227 g
3 tablespoons bourbon	45 ml
1 (6 ounce) chocolate piecrust	168 g

- In saucepan on low heat, melt marshmallows in milk and stir constantly. (Do not boil.) Cool in refrigerator.

- Fold into whipped cream while adding bourbon and pour into piecrust. Refrigerate at least 5 hours before serving.

Chess Pie

½ cup (1 stick) butter, softened	120 ml
2 cups sugar	480 ml
1 tablespoon cornstarch	15 ml
4 eggs	
1 (9 inch) piecrust	23 cm

■ Preheat oven to 325° (162° C).

■ Cream butter, sugar and cornstarch. Add eggs one at a time and beat well after each addition.

■ Pour mixture into piecrust. (Cover piecrust edges with strips of foil to prevent excessive browning.)

■ Bake for 45 minutes or until center sets.

Peanut Butter Pie

⅔ cup crunchy peanut butter	160 ml
1 (8 ounce) package cream cheese, softened	227 g
½ cup milk	120 ml
1 cup powdered sugar	240 ml
1 (8 ounce) carton whipped topping	227 g
1 (9 ounce) graham cracker piecrust	255 g

■ With mixer, blend peanut butter, cream cheese, milk and powdered sugar and fold in whipped topping.

■ Pour into piecrust and refrigerate several hours before serving.

Peach-Mousse Pie

Incredibly good!

1 (16 ounce) package frozen peach slices, thawed	.5 kg
1 cup sugar	240 ml
1 (1 ounce) packet unflavored gelatin	28 g
⅛ teaspoon ground nutmeg	.5 ml
¾ (8 ounce) carton whipped topping	¾ (227 g)
1 (9 ounce) graham cracker piecrust	255 g

- Place peaches in blender and process until smooth.

- Transfer peaches to saucepan, bring to a boil and stir constantly.

- Combine sugar, gelatin and nutmeg and stir into hot puree until sugar and gelatin dissolve.

- Pour gelatin-peach mixture into large mixing bowl.

- Place in freezer until mixture mounds (about 20 minutes) and stir occasionally

- Beat mixture at high speed about 5 minutes until it becomes light and frothy.

- Fold in whipped topping and spoon into piecrust.

Strawberry-Cream Cheese Pie

2 (10 ounce) packages frozen, sweetened strawberries, thawed	2 (280 g)
2 (8 ounce) packages cream cheese, softened	2 (227 g)
⅔ cup powdered sugar	160 ml
1 (8 ounce) carton whipped topping	227 g
1 (6 ounce) chocolate crumb piecrust	168 g

- Drain strawberries and reserve ¼ cup (60 ml) juice.

- In mixing bowl, combine cream cheese, reserved juice, strawberries and sugar and beat well.

- Fold in whipped topping and spoon into piecrust.

- Refrigerate overnight and garnish with fresh strawberries.

Creamy Lemon Pie

1 (8 ounce) package cream cheese, softened	227 g
1 (14 ounce) can sweetened condensed milk	396 g
¼ cup lemon juice	60 ml
1 (20 ounce) can lemon pie filling	567 g
1 (9 ounce) graham cracker piecrust	255 g

- In mixing bowl, beat cream cheese until creamy.
- Add sweetened condensed milk and lemon juice and beat until mixture is very creamy.
- Fold in lemon pie filling, stir until creamy and pour into piecrust.
- Refrigerate several hours before slicing and serving.

Limeade Pie

1 (6 ounce) can frozen limeade concentrate, thawed	168 g
2 cups low-fat frozen yogurt, softened	480 ml
1 (8 ounce) carton whipped topping, thawed	227 g
1 (6 ounce) graham cracker piecrust	168 g

- In large mixing bowl, combine limeade concentrate and yogurt and mix well.
- Fold in whipped topping and pour into piecrust.
- Freeze for at least 4 hours or overnight.

Easy Cheesecake

2 (8 ounce) packages cream cheese, softened　2 (227 g)
½ cup sugar　　　　　　　　　　　　　　　120 ml
½ teaspoon vanilla extract　　　　　　　　　2 ml
2 eggs
1 (9 ounce) graham cracker piecrust　　　　　255 g

- Preheat oven to 350° (176° C).

- In mixing bowl, beat cream cheese, sugar, vanilla and eggs and pour into piecrust.

- Bake for 40 minutes.

- Cool and top with any flavor pie filling.

When you need a dessert in a hurry, buy a cheesecake and pour canned cherry pie filling over the top.

Old-Fashioned Applesauce Spice Cake

1 (18 ounce) box spice cake mix	510 g
3 eggs	
1¼ cups applesauce	300 ml
⅓ cup oil	80 ml
1 cup chopped pecans	240 ml

- Preheat oven to 350° (176° C).

- With mixer, combine cake mix, eggs, applesauce and oil and beat at medium speed for 2 minutes.

- Stir in pecans and pour into sprayed, floured 9 x 13-inch (23 x 33 cm) baking pan.

- Bake for 40 minutes or until toothpick inserted near center comes out clean. Cool.

- For frosting, use prepared vanilla frosting and add ½ teaspoon (2 ml) cinnamon.

Lemon-Pineapple Cake

1 (18 ounce) box lemon cake mix	510 g
1 (20 ounce) can crushed pineapple with juice	567 g
3 eggs	
⅓ cup oil	80 ml

- Preheat oven to 350° (176° C).

- In mixing bowl, combine all cake ingredients. Blend on low speed to moisten and beat on medium for 2 minutes.

- Pour batter into sprayed, floured 9 x 13-inch (23 x 33 cm) baking pan.

- Bake for 30 minutes. Cake is done when toothpick inserted in center comes out clean. (While cake is baking, prepare topping.) Cool for 15 minutes.

Lemon-Pineapple Cake Topping:

1 (14 ounce) can sweetened condensed milk	396 g
1 cup sour cream	240 ml
¼ cup lemon juice	60 ml

- In medium bowl, combine all topping ingredients. Stir well to blend.

- Pour over warm cake. Chill.

Hawaiian Dream Cake

This looks like a lot of trouble to make, but it really isn't.
And it is a wonderful cake!

1 (18 ounce) box yellow cake mix	510 g
4 eggs	
¾ cup oil	180 ml
½ (20 ounce) can crushed pineapple	
with half juice	½ (567 g)

- Preheat oven to 350° (176° C).

- With mixer, beat all ingredients for 4 minutes. Pour into sprayed, floured 9 x 13-inch (23 x 33 cm) baking pan.

- Bake for 30 to 35 minutes or until cake tests done with toothpick. Cool and spread Coconut-Pineapple Icing over cake.

Coconut-Pineapple Icing:

½ (20 ounce) can crushed pineapple	
with half juice	½ (567 g)
½ cup (1 stick) butter	120 ml
1 (16 ounce) box powdered sugar	.5 kg
1 (6 ounce) can flaked coconut	168 g

- Heat pineapple and butter and boil for 2 minutes. Add powdered sugar and coconut.

- Punch holes in cake with knife and pour hot icing over cake.

Two-Surprise Cake

The first surprise is how easy it is and the second surprise is how good it is! You'll make this more than once.

1 bakery orange-chiffon cake	
1 (15 ounce) can crushed pineapple with juice	425 g
1 (3.4 ounce) package instant vanilla pudding mix	100 g
1 (8 ounce) carton whipped topping	227 g
½ cup slivered almonds, toasted	120 ml

- Slice cake horizontally into 3 equal layers.

- Mix pineapple, pudding mix and whipped topping and blend well.

- Spread pineapple mixture onto each cake layer and top of cake. Sprinkle almonds on top and chill.

Strawberry Pound Cake

1 (18 ounce) box strawberry cake mix	510 g
1 (3.4 ounce) package instant pineapple pudding mix	100 g
⅓ cup oil	80 ml
4 eggs	
1 (3 ounce) package strawberry gelatin	84 g

- Preheat oven to 325° (162° C).

- Mix all ingredients plus 1 cup water and beat for 2 minutes at medium speed.

- Pour into sprayed, floured bundt pan.

- Bake for 55 to 60 minutes. Cake is done when toothpick inserted near center comes out clean.

- Cool for 20 minutes before removing cake from pan. If you would like an icing, use commercial vanilla icing.

TIP: If you like coconut better than pineapple, use coconut cream pudding mix instead of pineapple.

Coconut Cake Deluxe

This is a fabulous cake!

1 (18 ounce) box yellow cake mix	510 g
1 (14 ounce) can sweetened condensed milk	396 g
1 (15 ounce) can coconut cream	425 g
1 (3 ounce) can flaked coconut	84 g
1 (8 ounce) carton whipped topping	227 g

- Preheat oven to 350° (176° C).

- Mix cake batter according to package directions.

- Pour batter into sprayed, floured 9 x 13-inch (23 x 33 cm) baking pan and bake for 30 to 35 minutes or until toothpick inserted in center comes out clean.

- While cake is warm, punch holes in cake about 2 inches (5 cm) apart.

- Pour sweetened condensed milk over cake and spread until all milk soaks into cake.

- Pour coconut cream over cake and sprinkle with coconut.

- Cool, frost with whipped topping and chill.

Oreo Cake

1 (18 ounce) box white cake mix	510 g
⅓ cup oil	80 ml
4 egg whites	
1¼ cup coarsely chopped Oreo® cookies	300 ml

- Preheat oven to 350° (176° C). In mixing bowl, combine cake mix, oil, egg whites and 1¼ cups (300 ml) water.

- Blend on low speed until moist and then beat for 2 minutes at high speed. Gently fold in coarsely chopped cookies and pour batter into 2 sprayed, floured 8-inch (20 cm) round cake pans.

- Bake for 25 to 30 minutes or until toothpick inserted in center comes out clean. Cool for 15 minutes and remove from pan. Cool completely and frost.

Oreo Cake Frosting:

4¼ cups powdered sugar	1.1 L
1 cup (2 sticks) butter, softened	240 ml
1 cup shortening	240 ml
1 teaspoon almond extract	5 ml
½ cup crushed Oreo® cookies	120 ml

- With mixer, combine all frosting ingredients and beat until creamy. Frost first layer of cake, place second layer on top and frost top and sides. Sprinkle cookie crumbs over top.

- Do not use butter-flavored shortening.

Chocolate-Cherry Cake

This is a chocolate lover's dream.

1 (18 ounce) box milk chocolate cake mix	510 g
1 (20 ounce) can cherry pie filling	567 g
3 eggs	

- Preheat oven to 350° (176° C).

- In mixing bowl, combine cake mix, pie filling and eggs.

- Mix by hand and pour into sprayed, floured 9 x 13-inch (23 x 33 cm) baking dish.

- Bake for 35 to 40 minutes. Cake is done when toothpick inserted in center comes out clean.

Chocolate-Cherry Cake Frosting:

5 tablespoons (⅔ stick) butter	75 ml
1¼ cups sugar	300 ml
½ cup milk	120 ml
1 (6 ounce) package chocolate chips	168 g

- When cake is done, combine butter, sugar and milk in medium saucepan.

- Boil 1 minute and stir constantly.

- Add chocolate chips and stir until chips melt.

- Pour over hot cake.

Twinkie Dessert

1 (10 count) box twinkies
4 bananas, sliced
1 (5 ounce) package instant vanilla pudding mix   143 g
1 (20 ounce) can crushed pineapple, drained   567 g
1 (8 ounce) carton whipped topping   227 g

- Slice twinkies in half lengthwise and place in sprayed 9 x 13-inch (23 x 33 cm) pan cream-side up.

- Make layer of sliced bananas.

- Prepare pudding according to package directions (use 2 cups/480 ml milk).

- Pour pudding over bananas and add pineapple.

- Top with whipped topping and refrigerate.

- Cut into squares to serve.

Sometimes the simplest of ideas will make the best desserts. If you're hungry for something sweet or have unexpected guests, you can't go wrong with canned pie-filling poured over ready-made cake and topped with whipped topping.

Strawberry Trifle

1 (5 ounce) package instant French vanilla pudding mix	143 g
1 (12 ounce) prepared bakery pound cake, sliced	340 g
2 cups fresh strawberries, sliced	480 ml
½ cup sherry	120 ml
Whipped topping	

- Prepare pudding according to package directions.
- Place layer of pound cake slices in 8-inch (20 cm) crystal bowl and sprinkle with ¼ cup (60 ml) sherry.
- Layer half of strawberries and half pudding on top.
- Repeat all layers and chill overnight or several hours.
- Before serving, top with whipped topping.

Peachy Sundaes

1 pint vanilla ice cream	.5 kg
¾ cup peach preserves, warmed	180 ml
¼ cup chopped almonds, toasted	180 ml
¼ cup flaked coconut	180 ml

- Divide ice cream into 4 sherbet dishes.

- Top with preserves.

- Sprinkle with almonds and coconut.

Mango Cream

2 soft mangoes	
½ gallon vanilla ice cream, softened	2 L
1 (6 ounce) can frozen lemonade concentrate, thawed	168 g
1 (8 ounce) carton whipped topping	227 g

- Peel mangoes, cut slices around seeds and cut into small chunks.

- In large bowl, mix ice cream, lemonade concentrate and whipped topping and fold in mango chunks.

- Quickly spoon mixture into parfait or sherbet glasses and cover with plastic wrap.

- Place in freezer.

Butterscotch Finale

1 (16 ounce) carton whipping cream	.5 kg
¾ cup butterscotch ice cream topping	180 ml
1 (14 ounce) prepared angel food cake	396 g
¾ pound toffee bars, crushed, divided	340 g

- In mixing bowl, whip cream until thick.

- Slowly add butterscotch topping and continue to beat until mixture is thick.

- Slice cake horizontally into 3 equal layers.

- Place bottom layer on cake plate, spread with 1½ cups (360 ml) whipped cream mixture and sprinkle with one-fourth crushed toffee.

- Repeat layers and frost top and sides of cake with remaining whipped cream mixture.

- Sprinkle toffee over top of cake. Chill for at least 8 hours before serving.

Keeping an angel food cake in the freezer will make you look like a kitchen pro when it comes time to prepare a last-minute dessert. You can top cake with fresh berries, pie filling, ice cream, chocolate syrup, butterscotch syrup, caramel sauce and always whipped topping.

Ice Cream Dessert

18 ice cream sandwiches
1 (12 ounce) carton whipped topping, thawed   340 g
1 (12 ounce) jar hot fudge ice cream topping   340 g
1 cup salted peanuts   240 ml

- Cut 1 ice cream sandwich in half.

- Place 1 whole and 1 half sandwich along short side of unsprayed 9 x 13-inch (23 x 33 cm) pan.

- Arrange 8 sandwiches in opposite direction in pan.

- Spread with half whipped topping.

- Spoon fudge topping by teaspoonfuls onto whipped topping and sprinkle with ½ cup (120 ml) peanuts.

- Repeat layers with remaining ice cream sandwiches, whipped topping and peanuts. (Pan will be full.)

- Cover and freeze. Take out of freezer 20 minutes before serving.

When you need a dessert fast, try ice cream with liqueur poured over it.
Keep a bottle of almond-flavored liqueur (Amaretto), coffee-flavored liqueur
(Kahlua), raspberry-flavored liqueur (Chambord) or your favorite flavored
drink. It's so fast and easy! And it tastes really special.

Blueberry-Angel Dessert

1 (8 ounce) package cream cheese, softened   227 g
1 cup powdered sugar   240 ml
1 (8 ounce) carton whipped topping, thawed   227 g
1 (14 ounce) prepared bakery angel food cake   396 g
2 (20 ounce) cans blueberry pie filling   2 (567 g)

- In large mixing bowl, beat cream cheese and powdered sugar and fold in whipped topping.

- Tear cake into small 1 or 2-inch (2.5 cm) cubes and fold into cream cheese mixture.

- Spread mixture evenly in 9 x 13-inch (23 x 33 cm) dish and top with pie filling.

- Cover and refrigerate for at least 3 hours before cutting into squares to serve.

Blueberry Fluff

1 (20 ounce) can blueberry pie filling	567 g
1 (20 ounce) can crushed pineapple, drained	567 g
1 (14 ounce) can sweetened condensed milk	396 g
1 (8 ounce) carton whipped topping	227 g

- Mix pie filling, pineapple and sweetened condensed milk.

- Fold in whipped topping. (This dessert is even better if you add ¾ cup/180 ml chopped pecans.)

- Pour into parfait glasses and chill.

Brandied Fruit

2 (20 ounce) cans crushed pineapple	2 (567 g)
1 (16 ounce) can sliced peaches	.5 kg
2 (11 ounce) cans mandarin oranges	2 (312 g)
1 (10 ounce) jar maraschino cherries	280 g
Sugar	
1 cup brandy	240 ml

- Let all fruit drain for 12 hours.

- For every cup of drained fruit, add ½ cup (120 ml) sugar. Let stand 12 hours.

- Add brandy, spoon into large jar and store in refrigerator. This mixture needs to stand in refrigerator for 3 weeks.

- Serve over ice cream.

Fun Fruit Fajitas

1 (20 ounce) can cherry pie filling	567 g
8 large flour tortillas	
1½ cups sugar	360 ml
¾ cup (1½ sticks) butter	180 ml
1 teaspoon almond flavoring	5 ml

- Divide fruit equally on tortillas, roll and place in 9 x 13-inch (23 x 33 cm) baking dish.

- Mix sugar and butter in saucepan with 2 cups (480 ml) water and bring to a boil.

- Add almond flavoring and pour sugar mixture over flour tortillas.

- Place in refrigerator and soak 1 to 24 hours.

- Bake at 350° (176° C) for 20 minutes or until brown and bubbly. Serve hot or room temperature.

TIP: Use any flavor of pie filling you like.

Amaretto Peaches

4½ cups peeled, sliced fresh peaches	1.1 L
½ cup Amaretto® liqueur	120 ml
½ cup sour cream	120 ml
½ cup packed brown sugar	120 ml

- Lay peaches in 2-quart (2 L) baking dish.
- Pour Amaretto® over peaches and spread with sour cream.
- Sprinkle brown sugar evenly over top.
- Broil mixture until it heats thoroughly and sugar melts.
- Serve over ice cream or pound cake.

Amaretto Ice Cream

1 (8 ounce) carton whipping cream, whipped	227 g
1 pint vanilla ice cream, softened	.5 kg
⅓ cup Amaretto® liqueur	80 ml
⅓ cup chopped almonds, toasted	80 ml

- Combine whipped cream, ice cream and Amaretto® and freeze in sherbet glasses.
- When ready to serve, drizzle a little additional amaretto over top of each individual serving and sprinkle with toasted almonds.

U.S. Measurements

3 teaspoons	1 tablespoon	
4 tablespoons	¼ cup	2 fluid ounces
8 tablespoons	½ cup	4 fluid ounces
12 tablespoons	¾ cup	6 fluid ounces
16 tablespoons	1 cup	8 fluid ounces
¼ cup	4 tablespoons	2 fluid ounces
⅓ cup	5 tablespoons + 1 teaspoon	
½ cup	8 tablespoons	4 fluid ounces
⅔ cup	10 tablespoons + 2 teaspoons	
¾ cup	12 tablespoons	6 fluid ounces
1 cup	16 tablespoons	8 fluid ounces
1 cup	½ pint	
2 cups	1 pint	16 fluid ounces
3 cups	1½ pints	24 fluid ounces
4 cups	1 quart	32 fluid ounces
8 cups	2 quarts	64 fluid ounces
1 pint	2 cups	16 fluid ounces
2 pints	1 quart	
1 quart	2 pints; 4 cups	32 fluid ounces
4 quarts	1 gallon; 8 pints; 16 cups	
8 quarts	1 peck	
4 pecks	1 bushel	

Cake Pans

5 x 2 round	2⅔ cups
6 x 2 round	3¾ cups
8 x 1.5 round	4 cups
7 x 2 round	5¼ cups
8 x 2 round	6 cups
9 x 1.5 round	6 cups
9 x 2 round	8 cups
9 x 3 bundt	9 cups
10 x 3.5 bundt	12 cups
9.5 x 2.5 springform	10 cups
10 x 2.5 springform	12 cups
8 x 3 tube	9 cups
9 x 4 tube	11 cups
10 x 4 tube	16 cups

Casseroles

8 x 8 x 12 square	8 cups
11 x 7 x 12 rectangular	8 cups
9 x 9 x 2 square	10 cups
13 x 9 x 2 rectangular	15 cups
1-quart casserole	4 cups
2-quart casserole	8 cups
2.5 quart casserole	10 cups
3-quart casserole	12 cups

Grocery List for
Busy Woman's Quick 'n Easy

Fresh Produce
____ Apples
____ Avocados
____ Bananas
____ Beans
____ Bell Peppers
____ Broccoli
____ Cabbage
____ Carrots
____ Cauliflower
____ Celery
____ Corn
____ Cucumbers
____ Garlic
____ Grapefruit
____ Grapes
____ Lemons
____ Lettuce
____ Lime
____ Melons
____ Mushrooms
____ Onions
____ Oranges
____ Peaches
____ Pears
____ Peppers
____ Potatoes
____ Strawberries
____ Spinach
____ Squash
____ Tomatoes
____ Zucchini
____ _____
____ _____

Deli
____ Cheese
____ Chicken
____ Turkey
____ Ham
____ Main Dish
____ Prepared Salad
____ Sandwich Meat
____ Side Dish
____ _____

Fresh Bakery
____ Bagels
____ Bread
____ Cake
____ Cookies
____ Croissants
____ Donuts
____ French Bread
____ Muffins
____ Pastries
____ Pies
____ Rolls

Dairy
____ Biscuits
____ Butter
____ Cheese
____ Cottage Cheese
____ Cream Cheese
____ Cream
____ Creamer
____ Eggs
____ Juice
____ Margarine
____ Milk
____ Pudding
____ Sour Cream
____ Yogurt
____ _____
____ _____

Frozen Foods
____ Breakfast
____ Dinners
____ Ice
____ Ice Cream
____ Juice
____ Pastries
____ Pies
____ Pizza
____ Potatoes
____ Vegetables
____ Whipping Cream
____ Whipped Topping

Grocery List for
Busy Woman's Quick 'n Easy

Grocery
___ Beans
___ Beer/Wine
___ Bread
___ Canned Vegetables
___ _____
___ _____
___ Cereal
___ Chips/Snacks
___ Coffee
___ Cookies
___ Crackers
___ Flour
___ Honey
___ Jelly
___ Juice
___ Ketchup
___ Kool-Aid
___ Mayonnaise
___ Mixes
___ _____
___ _____
___ Mustard
___ Nuts/Seeds
___ Oil
___ Pasta
___ Peanut Butter
___ Pickles/Olives
___ Popcorn
___ Rice
___ Salad Dressing
___ Salt
___ Seasonings
___ _____
___ _____
___ Sauce
___ Sodas
___ Soups
___ Spices
___ _____
___ _____
___ Sugar
___ Syrup
___ Tea
___ Tortillas
___ Water
___ _____
___ _____

Meat
___ Bacon
___ Chicken
___ Ground Beef
___ Ham
___ Hot Dogs
___ Pork
___ Roast
___ Sandwich Meat
___ Sausage
___ Steak
___ Turkey
___ _____
___ _____

General Merchandise
___ Automotive
___ Baby Items
___ _____
___ Bath Soap
___ Bath Tissue
___ Deodorant
___ Detergent
___ Dish Soap
___ Facial Tissue
___ Feminine Products
___ Aluminum Foil
___ Greeting Cards
___ Hardware
___ Insecticides
___ Light Bulbs
___ Lotion
___ Medicine
___ Napkins
___ Paper Plates
___ Paper Towels
___ Pet Supplies
___ Prescriptions
___ Shampoo
___ Toothpaste
___ Vitamins
___ _____
___ _____

Food Substitutions

You Need:	Use Instead:
1 cup breadcrumbs	¾ cup cracker crumbs
1 cup butter	⅞ cup vegetable oil or shortening
1 cup buttermilk	1 cup whole milk plus 1 tablespoon vinegar or lemon juice; or 1 cup plain yogurt
1 ounce unsweetened chocolate	3 tablespoons unsweetened cocoa plus 1 tablespoon butter
1 tablespoon corn starch	2 tablespoons all-purpose flour
1 cup cracker crumbs	1¼ cups breadcrumbs
1 cup cake flour	1 cup, less 2 tablespoons all-purpose flour
1 clove garlic	1 teaspoon garlic salt less ½ teaspoon salt in recipe
1 tablespoon fresh herbs	1 teaspoon dried herbs
1 cup whole milk	½ cup evaporated milk plus ½ cup water; or ¾ cup nonfat milk plus ¼ cup butter
1 tablespoon prepared mustard	1 teaspoon dry mustard
1 small onion	1 tablespoon minced onion; or ½ teaspoon onion powder
1 cup sour cream	1 cup plain yogurt; or 1 tablespoon lemon juice plus enough evaporated whole milk to equal 1 cup
1 cup sugar	1¾ cups powdered sugar; or 1 cup packed brown sugar
1 cup powdered sugar	½ cup plus 1 tablespoon granulated sugar
1 cup tomato juice	½ cup tomato sauce plus ½ cup water
1 cup tomato sauce	½ cup tomato paste plus ½ cup water
1 cup yogurt	1 cup milk plus 1 tablespoon lemon juice

Index

A

Across-the-Border Tamale Soup 70
After-Thanksgiving Turkey Chili 182
Alfredo Chicken 152
Amaretto Ice Cream 263
Amaretto Peaches 263
Appetizers
  Chunky Shrimp Dip 12
  Crab Dip Kick 24
  Creamy Cucumber Spread 24
  Creamy Ham Dip 15
  Creamy Onion Dip 23
  Creamy Spinach-Pepper Dip 22
  Crunchy Asparagus Dip 9
  Favorite Stand-By Shrimp Dip 23
  Fiesta Dip 8
  Horsey Shrimp Dip 10
  Hot Artichoke Spread 14
  Hot Broccoli Dip 9
  Hot Cocktail Squares 18
  Hot Rich Crab Dip 13
  Hot Sombrero Dip 11
  Nutty Apple Dip 15
  Olive-Cheese Balls 21
  Onion-Guacamole Dip 8
  Party Smokies 20
  Roasted Garlic Dip 25
  Sausage-Pineapple Bits 19
  Sausage Bites 20
  Speedy Chili Con Queso 19
  Spinach-Artichoke Dip 21
  Tasty Tuna Dip 14
  Tuna Melt Appetizer 17
  Unbelievable Crab Dip 13
  Vegetable Dip 11
  Velvet Clam Dip 12
  Walnut-Cheese Spread 18
  Zippy Broccoli-Cheese Dip 16

Apple
  Apple-Pineapple Salad 97
  Broccoli-Waldorf Salad 93
  Cranapple Wiggle 97
  Cranberry Chicken 160
  Green and Red Salad 86
  Nutty Apple Dip 15
  Old-Fashioned Applesauce Spice
      Cake 247
  Pork Chops and Apples 188
Apple-Pineapple Salad 97
Apricot-Baked Ham 194
Apricot-Pineapple Muffins 56
Apricot Bake 39
Apricot Bars 228
Apricot Chicken 170
Apricot Cobbler 238
Asian Beef and Noodles 137
Asparagus
  Asparagus-Cheese Chicken 181
  Asparagus Bake 123
  Crunchy Asparagus Dip 9
Asparagus-Cheese Chicken 181
Asparagus Bake 123
Aztec Creamy Salsa Chicken 154

B

Bacon-Cheese French Bread 58
Bacon-Egg Burrito 38
Bacon-Sour Cream Omelet 44
Bacon-Wrapped Chicken 179
Baked Beans 124
Baked Eggplant 117
Baked Fish 205
Baked Grits 48
Baked Halibut 211
Baked Ham and Pineapple 192
Baked Onion-Mushroom Steak 141
Baked Onions 113
Baked Oysters 217
Baked Rice 109

Baked Squash 118
Baked Tomatoes 116
Banana
Banana-Mango Smoothie 34
Lemon-Banana Shake 28
Reception Punch 32
Strawberry Smoothie 34
Banana-Mango Smoothie 34
Bars
Apricot Bars 228
Gooey Turtle Bars 227
Nutty Blonde Brownies 225
Pecan Squares 229
Snicker Brownies 226
Walnut Bars 229
Beans
Across-the-Border Tamale Soup 70
Beefy Bean Chili 73
Blue Norther Stew 72
Chili Casserole 128
Deluxe Dinner Nachos 148
Easy Chili 130
Fantastic Fried Corn 111
Fast Fiesta Soup 66
Fiesta Dip 8
Hearty Bean and Ham Soup 74
Navy Bean Soup 64
Pinto Beef Pie 131
Sausage-Vegetable Soup 79
Southwestern Bean Soup 83
Southwestern Soup 67
Sunshine Salad 91
Winter Salad 85
Beef
Across-the-Border Tamale Soup 70
Asian Beef and Noodles 137
Baked Onion-Mushroom Steak 141
Blue Norther Stew 72

Casserole Supper 129
Cheesy Beefy Gnocchi 128
Chili Casserole 128
Delicious Meatloaf 140
Easy Chili 130
Easy Winter Warmer 134
Lean Mean Round Steak 143
Meatball Soup 71
Next-Day Beef 146
Pepper Steak 135
Pinto Beef Pie 131
Potato-Beef Bake 139
Potato-Beef Casserole 129
Pot Roast 144
Ravioli and More 136
Red Wine Round Steak 142
Roasted Garlic Steak 144
Shepherds' Pie 138
Simple Spaghetti Bake 133
Slow Cookin', Good Tastin' Brisket 145
Smothered Beef Patties 138
Smothered Beef Steak 141
Smothered Steak 142
Southwestern Soup 67
Spanish Meatloaf 140
Speedy Vegetable Soup 67
Steak-Bake Italiano 130
Taco Pie 132
Beefy Bean Chili 73
Beer-Batter Shrimp 214
Best Tropical Punch 26
Beverages
Banana-Mango Smoothie 34
Best Tropical Punch 26
Champagne Punch 27
Cranberry-Pineapple Punch 26
Green Party Punch 31
Holiday Party Punch 30
Hot Cranberry Cider 28
Lemon-Banana Shake 28

Mexican Coffee 29
Orange Slush 27
Reception Punch 32
Sparkling Punch 33
Strawberry Punch 33
Strawberry Smoothie 34
Very Special Coffee Punch 29
Black Forest Pie 240
Blueberry-Angel Dessert 260
Blueberry Crunch 237
Blueberry Fluff 261
Blue Norther Stew 72
Boiled Shrimp 214
Brandied Fruit 261

Breads
Apricot-Pineapple Muffins 56
Bacon-Cheese French Bread 58
Caramel Rolls 55
Cheddar Cornbread 60
Cheese Drops 58
Cheesy Herb Bread 50
Cream Biscuits 53
Crunchy Breadsticks 59
Eagle Yeast Bread 57
French Onion Biscuits 56
Garlic Toast 50
Ham-Cheese Bars 62
Maple Syrup Biscuits 59
Mozzarella Loaf 60
Orange French Toast 53
Raspberry-Filled Blueberry
    Muffins 61
Souper-Sausage Cornbread 52
Spicy Cornbread Twists 52
Strawberry Bread 54

Breakfast & Brunch
Apricot-Pineapple Muffins 56
Apricot Bake 39
Bacon-Cheese French Bread 58
Bacon-Egg Burrito 38
Bacon-Sour Cream Omelet 44

Baked Grits 48
Breakfast Bake 36
Breakfast Tacos 37
Caramel Rolls 55
Cheddar Cornbread 60
Cheese Drops 58
Cheesy Herb Bread 50
Christmas Breakfast 46
Cinnamon Souffle 42
Cranberry Coffee Cake 45
Cream Biscuits 53
Crunchy Breadsticks 59
Curried Fruit Medley 39
Eagle Yeast Bread 57
French Onion Biscuits 56
Garlic Toast 50
Glazed Bacon 38
Green Chile Squares 47
Ham-Cheese Bars 62
Homemade Egg Substitute 47
Light, Crispy Waffles 43
Maple Syrup Biscuits 59
Mexican Breakfast Eggs 43
Mozzarella Loaf 60
Orange French Toast 53
Peach Bake 49
Pecan Waffles 46
Pineapple-Cheese Casserole 40
Pineapple Coffee Cake 44
Popovers 51
Praline Toast 48
Ranch Sausage-Grits 41
Raspberry-Filled Blueberry Muffins
    61
Salad Muffins 51
Souper-Sausage Cornbread 52
Sour Cream Biscuits 49
Spicy Cornbread Twists 52
Strawberry Bread 54
Breakfast Bake 36
Breakfast Tacos 37

Broccoli
  Alfredo Chicken 152
  Broccoli-Cheese Chicken 180
  Broccoli-Chicken Salad 95
  Broccoli-Noodle Salad 85
  Broccoli-Stuffed Tomatoes 116
  Broccoli-Waldorf Salad 93
  Broccoli-Wild Rice Soup 64
  Buttered Vegetables 110
  Chicken-Broccoli Chowder 68
  Chucky Clucky Casserole 149
  Corn Vegetable Medley 126
  Creamy Vegetable Casserole 125
  Crunchy Broccoli 115
  Incredible Broccoli-Cheese Soup
    82
  Parmesan Broccoli 115
  Zippy Broccoli-Cheese Dip 16
Broccoli-Cheese Chicken 180
Broccoli-Chicken Salad 95
Broccoli-Noodle Salad 85
Broccoli-Stuffed Tomatoes 116
Broccoli-Waldorf Salad 93
Broccoli-Wild Rice Soup 64
Brown Sugar Carrots 114
Brown Sugar Cookies 236
Butter-Mint Salad 89
Butter Cookies 235
Buttered Vegetables 110
Butterscotch Cookies 230
Butterscotch Finale 258

C

Cabbage-Ham Soup 76
Cake
  Chocolate-Cherry Cake 254
  Coconut Cake Deluxe 252
  Easy Cheesecake 246
  Hawaiian Dream Cake 249
  Lemon-Pineapple Cake 248
  Old-Fashioned Applesauce Spice
    Cake 247
  Strawberry Pound Cake 251
  Two-Surprise Cake 250
Calico Corn 126
Candy
  Diamond Fudge 224
  Dream Candy 222
  Microwave Fudge 225
  Microwave Pralines 221
  Peanut Brittle 223
  Pecan-Topped Toffee 220
  White Chocolate Fudge 223
Caramel Crunch 222
Caramel Rolls 55
Carrot Salad 92
Casserole Supper 129
Catalina Chicken 171
Cauliflower
  Cauliflower Medley 122
  Corn Vegetable Medley 126
  Creamy Vegetable Casserole 125
  Savory Cauliflower 121
  Veggie Salad 100
Cauliflower Medley 122
Champagne Punch 27
Cheddar Cornbread 60
Cheddar Potatoes 102
Cheese
  After-Thanksgiving Turkey Chili
    182
  Asparagus Bake 123
  Bacon-Cheese French Bread 58
  Bacon-Egg Burrito 38
  Baked Onions 113
  Baked Squash 118
  Breakfast Bake 36
  Breakfast Tacos 37
  Broccoli-Stuffed Tomatoes 116
  Broccoli-Wild Rice Soup 64
  Calico Corn 126

Cauliflower Medley 122
Cheddar Potatoes 102
Cheesy Chicken and Potatoes 182
Cheesy Herb Bread 50
Chicken Bake 174
Chicken Spaghetti 151
Chile-Cheese Squash 118
Chile-Chicken Roll-Ups 157
Chili Casserole 128
Chipper Fish 213
Christmas Breakfast 46
Chucky Clucky Casserole 149
Corn Vegetable Medley 126
Cottage Cheese-Fruit Salad 96
Crab Dip Kick 24
Crab Mornay 217
Creamed-Spinach Bake 120
Creamy Cabbage Bake 113
Creamy Cucumber Spread 24
Creamy Ham Dip 15
Creamy Onion Dip 23
Creamy Spinach-Pepper Dip 22
Creamy Vegetable Casserole 125
Deluxe Dinner Nachos 148
Divinity Salad 90
Easy Winter Warmer 134
Fiesta Dip 8
Fried Zucchini 117
Frozen Dessert Salad 99
Frozen Holiday Salad 98
Garlic Toast 50
Green Chile Squares 47
Grilled Chicken Cordon Bleu 165
Ham and Corn Chowder 77
Ham and Potatoes Olé! 198
Horsey Shrimp Dip 10
Hot Artichoke Spread 14
Hot Broccoli Dip 9
Hot Cocktail Squares 18
Hot Rich Crab Dip 13

Hot Sombrero Dip 11
Incredible Broccoli-Cheese Soup 82
Italian Chicken and Rice 165
Jiffy Chicken 176
Lean Mean Round Steak 143
Macaroni and Cheese 108
Mashed Potatoes Supreme 102
Mozzarella Cutlets 175
Nutty Apple Dip 15
Olive-Cheese Balls 21
Parmesan Broccoli 115
Parmesan Chicken Breasts 156
Pasta with Basil 107
Pepper Steak 135
Pink Salad 96
Potatoes au Gratin 103
Ranch Chicken 161
Ranch Sausage-Grits 41
Ravioli and More 136
Roasted Garlic Dip 25
Sandwich Souffle 196
Scalloped Potatoes 105
Shepherds' Pie 138
Shoe-Peg Corn Casserole 111
Simple Spaghetti Bake 133
Soup with an Attitude 75
Southwestern Bean Soup 83
Speedy Chili Con Queso 19
Spinach-Artichoke Dip 21
Spinach Casserole 121
Stuffed Cucumber Slices 93
Stuffed Yellow Squash 119
Taco Pie 132
Tuna Melt Appetizer 17
Twice-Baked Potatoes 106
Unbelievable Crab Dip 13
Walnut-Cheese Spread 18
Walnut-Ham Linguine 195
Zippy Broccoli-Cheese Dip 16
Zucchini Bake 119

Cheese Drops 58
Cheesy Beefy Gnocchi 128
Cheesy Chicken and Potatoes 182
Cheesy Herb Bread 50
Cherry Cobbler 239
Cherry Cranberry Salad 90
Cherry Crisp 237
Cherry Salad 89
Chess Pie 242

Chicken
  Alfredo Chicken 152
  Apricot Chicken 170
  Asparagus-Cheese Chicken 181
  Aztec Creamy Salsa Chicken 154
  Bacon-Wrapped Chicken 179
  Broccoli-Cheese Chicken 180
  Broccoli-Chicken Salad 95
  Catalina Chicken 171
  Cheesy Chicken and Potatoes 182
  Chicken-Broccoli Chowder 68
  Chicken and Wild Rice Special 162
  Chicken Bake 174
  Chicken Chow Mein 150
  Chicken Quesadillas 158
  Chicken Salad 87
  Chile-Chicken Roll-Ups 157
  Chile Pepper Chicken 170
  Chucky Clucky Casserole 149
  Cola Chicken 158
  Cranberry Chicken 160
  Crispy Nutty Chicken 171
  Crunchy Chip Chicken 159
  Dad's Best Smoked Chicken 164
  Deluxe Dinner Nachos 148
  Favorite Chicken Breasts 173
  Finger Lickin' BBQ Chicken 155
  Grilled Chicken Cordon Bleu 165
  Hawaiian Chicken 169
  Honey-Baked Chicken 177
  Italian Chicken and Rice 165
  Jiffy Chicken 176

Lemonade Chicken 163
Lemony Chicken and Noodles 166
Mozzarella Cutlets 175
One-Dish Chicken Bake 172
Parmesan Chicken Breasts 156
Party Chicken Breasts 163,178
Quickie Russian Chicken 153
Ranch Chicken 161
Spicy Chicken and Rice 160
Stir-Fry Chicken Spaghetti 168
Sunday Chicken 161
Sweet-and-Sour Chicken 167
Chicken-Broccoli Chowder 68
Chicken and Wild Rice Special 162
Chicken Bake 174
Chicken Chow Mein 150
Chicken Quesadillas 158
Chicken Salad 87
Chicken Spaghetti 151
Chile-Cheese Squash 118
Chile-Chicken Roll-Ups 157
Chile Pepper Chicken 170

Chili
  Beefy Bean Chili 73
  Easy Chili 130
Chili Casserole 128
Chinese Cookies 230
Chipper Fish 213
Chips and Fish 206

Chocolate
  Chinese Cookies 230
  Chocolate-Cherry Cake 254
  Coconut Yummies 231
  Devil's Food Cookies 236
  Diamond Fudge 224
  Dixie Pie 241
  Easy Chocolate Pie 241
  Gooey Turtle Bars 227
  Ice Cream Dessert 259
  Microwave Fudge 225
  Oreo Cake 253

Pecan-Topped Toffee 220
Snicker Brownies 226
White Chocolate Fudge 223
Chocolate-Cherry Cake 254
Chowder
Chicken-Broccoli Chowder 68
Clam Chowder 76
Ham and Corn Chowder 77
Rich Corn Chowder 78
Christmas Breakfast 46
Chucky Clucky Casserole 149
Chunky Shrimp Dip 12
Cinnamon Souffle 42
Clam Chowder 76
Coconut Cake Deluxe 252
Coconut Macaroons 235
Coconut Yummies 231
Cola Chicken 158
Color-Coded Salad 94
Cookies
Brown Sugar Cookies 236
Butter Cookies 235
Butterscotch Cookies 230
Chinese Cookies 230
Coconut Macaroons 235
Coconut Yummies 231
Devil's Food Cookies 236
Haystacks 231
Orange Balls 232
Peanut Butter Crunchies 232
Pecan Puffs 234
Sand Tarts 233
Scotch Shortbread 233
Corn
Across-the-Border Tamale Soup 70
Blue Norther Stew 72
Buttered Vegetables 110
Calico Corn 126
Corn Vegetable Medley 126
Deluxe Dinner Nachos 148

Fantastic Fried Corn 111
Fast Fiesta Soup 66
Ham and Corn Chowder 77
Rich Corn Chowder 78
Shepherds' Pie 138
Shoe-Peg Corn Casserole 111
Simple Spaghetti Bake 133
Southwestern Soup 67
Sunshine Salad 91
Winter Salad 85
Corn Vegetable Medley 126
Cottage Cheese-Fruit Salad 96
Crab
Crabmeat Casserole 216
Crab Mornay 217
Hot Rich Crab Dip 13
Seafood Bisque 80
Super Easy Gumbo 79
Unbelievable Crab Dip 13
Crab Dip Kick 24
Crabmeat Casserole 216
Crab Mornay 217
Cranapple Wiggle 97
Cranberry
Cherry Cranberry Salad 90
Cranapple Wiggle 97
Cranberry-Pineapple Punch 26
Cranberry Chicken 160
Cranberry Coffee Cake 45
Frozen Holiday Salad 98
Hot Cranberry Cider 28
Nutty Cranberry Relish 94
Cranberry-Pineapple Punch 26
Cranberry Chicken 160
Cranberry Coffee Cake 45
Cream Biscuits 53
Creamed-Spinach Bake 120
Creamed Green Peas 112
Creamed Shrimp Over Rice 215
Cream of Zucchini Soup 65
Creamy Cucumber Spread 24

Creamy Fettuccine 108
Creamy Ham Dip 15
Creamy Lemon Pie 245
Creamy Onion Dip 23
Creamy Spinach-Pepper Dip 22
Creamy Turkey Soup 69
Creamy Vegetable Casserole 125
Crispy Fish and Cheese Filets 204
Crispy Nutty Chicken 171
Crunchy Asparagus Dip 9
Crunchy Breadsticks 59
Crunchy Broccoli 115
Crunchy Chip Chicken 159
Curried Fruit Medley 39

D

Dad's Best Smoked Chicken 164
Delicious Meatloaf 140
Deluxe Dinner Nachos 148
Desserts
Amaretto Ice Cream 263
Amaretto Peaches 263
Apricot Bars 228
Apricot Cobbler 238
Black Forest Pie 240
Blueberry-Angel Dessert 260
Blueberry Crunch 237
Blueberry Fluff 261
Brandied Fruit 261
Brown Sugar Cookies 236
Butter Cookies 235
Butterscotch Cookies 230
Butterscotch Finale 258
Caramel Crunch 222
Cherry Cobbler 239
Cherry Crisp 237
Chess Pie 242
Chinese Cookies 230
Chocolate-Cherry Cake 254
Coconut Cake Deluxe 252
Coconut Macaroons 235

Coconut Yummies 231
Creamy Lemon Pie 245
Devil's Food Cookies 236
Diamond Fudge 224
Dixie Pie 241
Dream Candy 222
Easy Cheesecake 246
Easy Chocolate Pie 241
Easy Pumpkin Pie 239
Frozen Dessert Salad 99
Fun Fruit Fajitas 262
Gooey Turtle Bars 227
Hawaiian Dream Cake 249
Haystacks 231
Ice Cream Dessert 259
Lemon-Pineapple Cake 248
Limeade Pie 245
Mango Cream 257
Microwave Fudge 225
Microwave Pralines 221
Nutty Blonde Brownies 225
Old-Fashioned Applesauce Spice
     Cake 247
Orange Balls 232
Peach-Mousse Pie 243
Peachy Sundaes 257
Peanut Brittle 223
Peanut Butter Crunchies 232
Peanut Butter Pie 242
Pecan-Topped Toffee 220
Pecan Puffs 234
Pecan Squares 229
Pistachio Salad or Dessert 95
Sand Tarts 233
Scotch Shortbread 233
Snicker Brownies 226
Strawberry-Cream Cheese Pie 244
Strawberry Trifle 256
Twinkie Dessert 255
Two-Surprise Cake 250
Walnut Bars 229

White Chocolate Fudge 223
Devil's Food Cookies 236
Deviled Eggs 91
Diamond Fudge 224
Divinity Salad 90
Dixie Pie 241
Dream Candy 222

E

Eagle Yeast Bread 57
Easy Cheesecake 246
Easy Chili 130
Easy Chocolate Pie 241
Easy Potato Soup 66
Easy Pumpkin Pie 239
Easy Winter Warmer 134

F

Fantastic Fried Corn 111
Fantastic Fruit Salad 88
Fast Fiesta Soup 66
Favorite Chicken Breasts 173
Favorite Stand-By Shrimp Dip 23
Fiesta Dip 8
Finger Lickin' BBQ Chicken 155
Flounder au Gratin 208
French Onion Biscuits 56
Fresh Oyster Stew 81
Fried Zucchini 117
Frozen Dessert Salad 99
Frozen Holiday Salad 98
Fun Fruit Fajitas 262

G

Garlic Toast 50
Glazed Bacon 38
Golden Catfish Filets 207
Gooey Turtle Bars 227
Green and Red Salad 86
Green Chile-Rice 109
Green Chile Squares 47

Green Party Punch 31
Grilled Chicken Cordon Bleu 165
Grilled Pork Loin 197

H

Ham-Cheese Bars 62
Ham and Corn Chowder 77
Ham and Potatoes Olé! 198
Hawaiian Aloha Pork 200
Hawaiian Chicken 169
Hawaiian Dream Cake 249
Haystacks 231
Hearty Bean and Ham Soup 74
Holiday Party Punch 30
Homemade Egg Substitute 47
Honey
   Honey-Baked Chicken 177
   Pineapple-Pork Chops 184
   Tangy Pork Chops 189
Honey-Baked Chicken 177
Horsey Shrimp Dip 10
Hot Artichoke Spread 14
Hot Broccoli Dip 9
Hot Cocktail Squares 18
Hot Cranberry Cider 28
Hot Rich Crab Dip 13
Hot Sombrero Dip 11

I

Ice Cream Dessert 259
Incredible Broccoli-Cheese Soup 82
Italian Chicken and Rice 165
Italian Minestrone 84

J

Jiffy Chicken 176

L

Lean Mean Round Steak 143
Lemon-Baked Fish 210
Lemon-Banana Shake 28

Lemon-Dill Filets 209
Lemon-Pineapple Cake 248
Lemonade Chicken 163
Lemonade Spareribs 199
Lemony Chicken and Noodles 166
Light, Crispy Waffles 43
Limeade Pie 245

M

Macaroni and Cheese 108
Mango Cream 257
Maple Syrup Biscuits 59
Mashed Potatoes Supreme 102
Meatball Soup 71
Mexican Breakfast Eggs 43
Mexican Coffee 29
Microwave Fudge 225
Microwave Pralines 221
Mozzarella Cutlets 175
Mozzarella Loaf 60

N

Navy Bean Soup 64
Next-Day Beef 146
Nuts
  Amaretto Ice Cream 263
  Apple-Pineapple Salad 97
  Apricot Cobbler 238
  Broccoli-Noodle Salad 85
  Broccoli-Waldorf Salad 93
  Butterscotch Cookies 230
  Caramel Crunch 222
  Caramel Rolls 55
  Cherry Cobbler 239
  Cherry Crisp 237
  Cherry Salad 89
  Chicken Chow Mein 150
  Chinese Cookies 230
  Cranapple Wiggle 97
  Cranberry Chicken 160
  Crispy Nutty Chicken 171

  Crunchy Asparagus Dip 9
  Devil's Food Cookies 236
  Divinity Salad 90
  Dream Candy 222
  Easy Chocolate Pie 241
  Frozen Holiday Salad 98
  Glazed Bacon 38
  Gooey Turtle Bars 227
  Haystacks 231
  Ice Cream Dessert 259
  Microwave Fudge 225
  Microwave Pralines 221
  Nutty Apple Dip 15
  Nutty Blonde Brownies 225
  Nutty Green Salad 86
  Old-Fashioned Applesauce Spice
    Cake 247
  One-Dish Pork and Peas 202
  Orange Balls 232
  Orange Pork Chops 185
  Peachy Sundaes 257
  Peanut Brittle 223
  Pecan-Topped Toffee 220
  Pecan Puffs 234
  Pecan Squares 229
  Pecan Waffles 46
  Pink Salad 96
  Pistachio Salad or Dessert 95
  Praline Ham 193
  Praline Toast 48
  Raspberry-Filled Blueberry Muffins
    61
  Sand Tarts 233
  Sweet Potatoes and Pecans 104
  Two-Surprise Cake 250
  Veggie Salad 100
  Walnut-Cheese Spread 18
  Walnut-Ham Linguine 195
  Walnut Bars 229
  White Chocolate Fudge 223
Nutty Apple Dip 15
Nutty Blonde Brownies 225

Nutty Cranberry Relish 94
Nutty Green Salad 86

O

Old-Fashioned Applesauce Spice
    Cake 247
Olive-Cheese Balls 21
One-Dish Chicken Bake 172
One-Dish Pork and Peas 202
Onion-Guacamole Dip 8
Onion-Smothered Pork Chops 190
Orange Balls 232
Orange French Toast 53
Orange Pork Chops 185
Orange Roughy with Peppers 212
Orange Slush 27
Oven-Pork Chops 184
Oven Fries 104
Oven Pork Chops 189

P

Parmesan Broccoli 115
Parmesan Chicken Breasts 156
Party Chicken Breasts 163,178
Party Smokies 20
Pasta with Basil 107
Peach-Mousse Pie 243
Peach Bake 49
Peachy Fruit Salad 88
Peachy Glazed Ham 191
Peachy Sundaes 257
Peanut Brittle 223
Peanut Butter Crunchies 232
Peanut Butter Pie 242
Pecan-Topped Toffee 220
Pecan Puffs 234
Pecan Squares 229
Pecan Waffles 46
Pepper Steak 135
Pies
  Black Forest Pie 240

Chess Pie 242
Creamy Lemon Pie 245
Dixie Pie 241
Easy Chocolate Pie 241
Easy Pumpkin Pie 239
Limeade Pie 245
Peach-Mousse Pie 243
Peanut Butter Pie 242
Shepherds' Pie 138
Strawberry-Cream Cheese Pie 244
Pineapple
  Apple-Pineapple Salad 97
  Baked Ham and Pineapple 192
  Best Tropical Punch 26
  Butter-Mint Salad 89
  Carrot Salad 92
  Cherry Salad 89
  Cinnamon Souffle 42
  Cottage Cheese-Fruit Salad 96
  Cranapple Wiggle 97
  Cranberry-Pineapple Punch 26
  Curried Fruit Medley 39
  Divinity Salad 90
  Fantastic Fruit Salad 88
  Frozen Dessert Salad 99
  Frozen Holiday Salad 98
  Green Party Punch 31
  Hawaiian Chicken 169
  Hawaiian Dream Cake 249
  Holiday Party Punch 30
  Peachy Fruit Salad 88
  Pineapple-Cheese Casserole 40
  Pineapple-Pork Chops 184
  Pineapple Coffee Cake 44
  Pineapple Sauce for Ham 198
  Pink Salad 96
  Pistachio Salad or Dessert 95
  Reception Punch 32
  Twinkie Dessert 255
Pineapple-Cheese Casserole 40
Pineapple-Pork Chops 184

Pineapple Coffee Cake 44
Pineapple Sauce for Ham 198
Pine Nut Green Beans 114
Pink Salad 96
Pinto Beef Pie 131
Pistachio Salad or Dessert 95
Popovers 51

Pork
  Apricot-Baked Ham 194
  Bacon-Cheese French Bread 58
  Bacon-Egg Burrito 38
  Bacon-Sour Cream Omelet 44
  Bacon-Wrapped Chicken 179
  Baked Beans 124
  Baked Ham and Pineapple 192
  Cabbage-Ham Soup 76
  Christmas Breakfast 46
  Creamy Ham Dip 15
  Fresh Oyster Stew 81
  Glazed Bacon 38
  Grilled Chicken Cordon Bleu 165
  Grilled Pork Loin 197
  Ham-Cheese Bars 62
  Ham and Corn Chowder 77
  Ham and Potatoes Olé! 198
  Hawaiian Aloha Pork 200
  Hearty Bean and Ham Soup 74
  Lemonade Spareribs 199
  Navy Bean Soup 64
  One-Dish Pork and Peas 202
  Onion-Smothered Pork Chops
      190
  Orange Pork Chops 185
  Oven-Pork Chops 184
  Oven Pork Chops 189
  Party Chicken Breasts 163
  Peachy Glazed Ham 191
  Pineapple-Pork Chops 184
  Pineapple Sauce for Ham 198
  Pork Casserole 187
  Pork Chops and Apples 188

Pork Chops in Cream Gravy 187
Potato-Sausage Soup 71
Praline Ham 193
Ranch Sausage-Grits 41
Rich Corn Chowder 78
Sandwich Souffle 196
Sausage Casserole 193
Souper-Sausage Cornbread 52
Soup with an Attitude 75
Spicy Pork Chops 186
Sweet-and-Sour Spareribs 201
Tangy Pork Chops 189
Tenderloin with Apricot Sauce 201
Tequila Baby-Back Ribs 200
Walnut-Ham Linguine 195
Pork Casserole 187
Pork Chops and Apples 188
Pork Chops in Cream Gravy 187
Potato-Beef Bake 139
Potato-Beef Casserole 129
Potato-Sausage Soup 71

Potatoes
  Cheddar Potatoes 102
  Cheesy Chicken and Potatoes 182
  Chicken-Broccoli Chowder 68
  Creamy Turkey Soup 69
  Easy Potato Soup 66
  Ham and Corn Chowder 77
  Ham and Potatoes Olé! 198
  Mashed Potatoes Supreme 102
  Oven Fries 104
  Pork Casserole 187
  Potato-Beef Bake 139
  Potato-Beef Casserole 129
  Potato-Sausage Soup 71
  Potatoes au Gratin 103
  Potatoes Supreme 103
  Pot Roast 144
  Rich Corn Chowder 78
  Scalloped Potatoes 105
  Seafood Bisque 80

Shepherds' Pie 138
Soup with an Attitude 75
Sweet Potatoes and Pecans 104
Twice-Baked Potatoes 106
Potatoes au Gratin 103
Potatoes Supreme 103
Pot Roast 144
Praline Ham 193
Praline Toast 48

Q

Quickie Russian Chicken 153

R

Ranch Chicken 161
Ranch Sausage-Grits 41
Raspberry-Filled Blueberry Muffins
    61
Ravioli and More 136
Reception Punch 32
Red Wine Round Steak 142
Rice
    Baked Rice 109
    Broccoli-Wild Rice Soup 64
    Casserole Supper 129
    Chicken and Wild Rice Special
        162
    Creamed Shrimp Over Rice 215
    Green Chile-Rice 109
    Italian Chicken and Rice 165
    Special Rice Salad 87
    Speedy Vegetable Soup 67
    Spicy Chicken and Rice 160
Rich Corn Chowder 78
Roasted Garlic Dip 25
Roasted Garlic Steak 144
Roasted Vegetables 110

Salad Muffins 51

Salads
    Apple-Pineapple Salad 97
    Broccoli-Chicken Salad 95
    Broccoli-Noodle Salad 85
    Broccoli-Waldorf Salad 93
    Butter-Mint Salad 89
    Carrot Salad 92
    Cherry Cranberry Salad 90
    Cherry Salad 89
    Chicken Salad 87
    Color-Coded Salad 94
    Cottage Cheese-Fruit Salad 96
    Cranapple Wiggle 97
    Divinity Salad 90
    Fantastic Fruit Salad 88
    Frozen Dessert Salad 99
    Frozen Holiday Salad 98
    Green and Red Salad 86
    Nutty Cranberry Relish 94
    Nutty Green Salad 86
    Peachy Fruit Salad 88
    Pink Salad 96
    Pistachio Salad or Dessert 95
    Special Rice Salad 87
    Stuffed Cucumber Slices 93
    Sunshine Salad 91
    Swiss Salad 92
    Veggie Salad 100
    Winter Salad 85
Salmon Croquets 218
Sand Tarts 233
Sandwich Souffle 196
Sausage
    Breakfast Bake 36
    Christmas Breakfast 46
    Party Smokies 20
    Potato-Sausage Soup 71
    Ranch Sausage-Grits 41
    Sausage-Pineapple Bits 19
    Sausage-Vegetable Soup 79
    Sausage Bites 20

Sausage Casserole 193
Souper-Sausage Cornbread 52
Sausage-Pineapple Bits 19
Sausage-Vegetable Soup 79
Sausage Bites 20
Sausage Casserole 193
Savory Cauliflower 121
Scalloped Potatoes 105
Scotch Shortbread 233

Seafood
Baked Fish 205
Baked Halibut 211
Baked Oysters 217
Beer-Batter Shrimp 214
Boiled Shrimp 214
Chipper Fish 213
Chips and Fish 206
Chunky Shrimp Dip 12
Clam Chowder 76
Crabmeat Casserole 216
Crab Mornay 217
Creamed Shrimp Over Rice 215
Crispy Fish and Cheese Filets 204
Flounder au Gratin 208
Fresh Oyster Stew 81
Golden Catfish Filets 207
Horsey Shrimp Dip 10
Hot Rich Crab Dip 13
Lemon-Baked Fish 210
Lemon-Dill Filets 209
Orange Roughy with Peppers 212
Salmon Croquets 218
Seafood Bisque 80
Seafood Delight 215
Tasty Tuna Dip 14
Tuna and Chips 216
Tuna Melt Appetizer 17
Unbelievable Crab Dip 13
Velvet Clam Dip 12
Seafood Bisque 80
Seafood Delight 215

Sesame Asparagus 123
Shepherds' Pie 138
Shoe-Peg Corn Casserole 111
Shrimp
Beer-Batter Shrimp 214
Boiled Shrimp 214
Chunky Shrimp Dip 12
Creamed Shrimp Over Rice 215
Seafood Bisque 80

Side Dishes
Asparagus Bake 123
Baked Beans 124
Baked Eggplant 117
Baked Onions 113
Baked Rice 109
Baked Squash 118
Baked Tomatoes 116
Broccoli-Stuffed Tomatoes 116
Brown Sugar Carrots 114
Buttered Vegetables 110
Calico Corn 126
Cauliflower Medley 122
Cheddar Potatoes 102
Chile-Cheese Squash 118
Corn Vegetable Medley 126
Creamed-Spinach Bake 120
Creamed Green Peas 112
Creamy Cabbage Bake 113
Creamy Fettuccine 108
Creamy Vegetable Casserole 125
Crunchy Broccoli 115
Fantastic Fried Corn 111
Fried Zucchini 117
Green Chile-Rice 109
Macaroni and Cheese 108
Mashed Potatoes Supreme 102
Oven Fries 104
Parmesan Broccoli 115
Pasta with Basil 107
Pine Nut Green Beans 114
Potatoes au Gratin 103

Potatoes Supreme 103
Roasted Vegetables 110
Savory Cauliflower 121
Scalloped Potatoes 105
Sesame Asparagus 123
Shoe-Peg Corn Casserole 111
Spinach Casserole 121
Stuffed Yellow Squash 119
Sweet Potatoes and Pecans 104
Tasty Black-Eyed Peas 112
Twice-Baked Potatoes 106
Zucchini Bake 119
Simple Spaghetti Bake 133
Slow Cookin', Good Tastin' Brisket 145
Smothered Beef Patties 138
Smothered Beef Steak 141
Smothered Steak 142
Snicker Brownies 226
Souper-Sausage Cornbread 52

Soups

Across-the-Border Tamale Soup 70
Broccoli-Wild Rice Soup 64
Cabbage-Ham Soup 76
Cream of Zucchini Soup 65
Creamy Turkey Soup 69
Easy Potato Soup 66
Fast Fiesta Soup 66
Hearty Bean and Ham Soup 74
Incredible Broccoli-Cheese Soup 82
Meatball Soup 71
Navy Bean Soup 64
Potato-Sausage Soup 71
Sausage-Vegetable Soup 79
Soup with an Attitude 75
Southwestern Soup 67
Speedy Vegetable Soup 67
Tomato-French Onion Soup 65

Soups & Salads

Across-the-Border Tamale Soup 70
Apple-Pineapple Salad 97
Beefy Bean Chili 73
Broccoli-Chicken Salad 95
Broccoli-Noodle Salad 85
Broccoli-Waldorf Salad 93
Broccoli-Wild Rice Soup 64
Butter-Mint Salad 89
Cabbage-Ham Soup 76
Carrot Salad 92
Cherry Cranberry Salad 90
Cherry Salad 89
Chicken-Broccoli Chowder 68
Chicken Salad 87
Clam Chowder 76
Color-Coded Salad 94
Cottage Cheese-Fruit Salad 96
Cranapple Wiggle 97
Cream of Zucchini Soup 65
Deviled Eggs 91
Divinity Salad 90
Easy Potato Soup 66
Fantastic Fruit Salad 88
Fast Fiesta Soup 66
Fresh Oyster Stew 81
Frozen Dessert Salad 99
Frozen Holiday Salad 98
Green and Red Salad 86
Ham and Corn Chowder 77
Hearty Bean and Ham Soup 74
Incredible Broccoli-Cheese Soup 82
Italian Minestrone 84
Meatball Soup 71
Navy Bean Soup 64
Nutty Cranberry Relish 94
Nutty Green Salad 86
Peachy Fruit Salad 88
Pink Salad 96
Pistachio Salad or Dessert 95

Potato-Sausage Soup 71
Rich Corn Chowder 78
Sausage-Vegetable Soup 79
Seafood Bisque 80
Soup with an Attitude 75
Southwestern Bean Soup 83
Southwestern Soup 67
Special Rice Salad 87
Speedy Vegetable Soup 67
Stuffed Cucumber Slices 93
Sunshine Salad 91
Super Easy Gumbo 79
Swiss Salad 92
Tomato-French Onion Soup 65
Veggie Salad 100
Winter Salad 85
Soup with an Attitude 75
Sour Cream Biscuits 49
Southwestern Bean Soup 83
Southwestern Soup 67
Spanish Meatloaf 140
Sparkling Punch 33
Special Rice Salad 87
Speedy Chili Con Queso 19
Speedy Vegetable Soup 67
Spicy Chicken and Rice 160
Spicy Cornbread Twists 52
Spicy Pork Chops 186

Spinach
Creamed-Spinach Bake 120
Creamy Spinach-Pepper Dip 22
Spinach-Artichoke Dip 21
Spinach Casserole 121
Stuffed Yellow Squash 119
Tuna Melt Appetizer 17
Vegetable Dip 11
Spinach-Artichoke Dip 21
Spinach Casserole 121
Steak-Bake Italiano 130

Stews
Blue Norther Stew 72

Fresh Oyster Stew 81
Stir-Fry Chicken Spaghetti 168

Strawberry
Fantastic Fruit Salad 88
Frozen Dessert Salad 99
Strawberry-Cream Cheese Pie 244
Strawberry Bread 54
Strawberry Pound Cake 251
Strawberry Punch 33
Strawberry Smoothie 34
Strawberry Trifle 256
Strawberry-Cream Cheese Pie 244
Strawberry Bread 54
Strawberry Punch 33
Strawberry Smoothie 34
Strawberry Trifle 256
Stuffed Cucumber Slices 93
Stuffed Yellow Squash 119
Sunday Chicken 161
Sunshine Salad 91
Super Easy Gumbo 79
Sweet-and-Sour Chicken 167
Sweet-and-Sour Spareribs 201
Sweet Potatoes and Pecans 104
Swiss Salad 92

T

Taco Pie 132
Tangy Pork Chops 189
Tasty Black-Eyed Peas 112
Tasty Tuna Dip 14
Tenderloin with Apricot Sauce 201
Tequila Baby-Back Ribs 200
Tomato-French Onion Soup 65

Tuna
Tasty Tuna Dip 14
Tuna and Chips 216
Tuna Melt Appetizer 17
Tuna and Chips 216
Tuna Melt Appetizer 17
Turkey

After-Thanksgiving Turkey Chili
  182
  Creamy Turkey Soup 69
Twice-Baked Potatoes 106
Twinkie Dessert 255
Two-Surprise Cake 250

U

Unbelievable Crab Dip 13

V

Vegetable Dip 11
Veggie Salad 100
Velvet Clam Dip 12
Very Special Coffee Punch 29

W

Walnut-Cheese Spread 18
Walnut-Ham Linguine 195
Walnut Bars 229

White Chocolate Fudge 223
Winter Salad 85

Z

Zippy Broccoli-Cheese Dip 16
Zucchini
  Color-Coded Salad 94
  Fried Zucchini 117
  Italian Minestrone 84
  Nutty Green Salad 86
  Ravioli and More 136
  Veggie Salad 100
  Zucchini Bake 119
Zucchini Bake 119

Enjoy these cookbooks by Cookbook Resources, LLC

The Best of Cooking with 3 Ingredients

The Ultimate Cooking with 4 Ingredients

Easy Cooking with 5 Ingredients

Diabetic Cooking with 4 Ingredients

Healthy Cooking with 4 Ingredients

Gourmet Cooking with 5 Ingredients

4-Ingredient Recipes for 30-Minute Meals

Essential 3-4-5 Ingredient Recipes

The Best 1001 Short, Easy Recipes

The Best 1001 Fast Easy Recipes

Easy Slow Cooker Cookbook

Easy One-Dish Meals

Easy Potluck Recipes

Easy Casseroles

Easy Desserts

Sunday Night Suppers

Easy Church Suppers

365 Easy Meals

365 Easy Chicken Recipes

365 Easy Soups and Stews

Quick Fixes with Cake Mixes

Kitchen Keepsakes/More Kitchen Keepsakes

Gifts for the Cookie Jar

All New Gifts for the Cookie Jar

Muffins In A Jar

Brownies In A Jar

Gifts in a Pickle Jar

The Big Bake Sale Cookbook

Classic Tex-Mex & Texas Cooking

Classic Southwest Cooking

Southern Family Favorites

Miss Sadie's Southern Cooking

The Great Canadian Cookbook

Texas Longhorn Cookbook

Cookbook 25 Years

The Best of Lone Star Legacy Cookbook

A Little Taste of Texas

A Little Taste of Texas II

Trophy Hunters' Wild Game Cookbook

Italian Family Cookbook

Old-Fashioned Cookies

Grandmother's Cookies

Quilters' Cooking Companion

Mother's Recipes

Recipe Keeper

Cookie Dough Secrets

Casseroles to the Rescue

Holiday Recipes

Mealtimes and Memories

Southwest Sizzler

Southwest Olé

Class Treats

Leaving Home

To Order: **Busy Woman's Quick & Easy Recipes**

Please send_____ hardcover copies @ $19.95 (U.S.) each $ _____
Texas residents add sales tax @ $1.65 each $ _____
Plus postage/handling @ $6.00 (1st copy) $ _____
$1.00 (each additional copy) $ _____

Check or Credit Card (Canada-credit card only)   Total $ _____

Charge to:
_____ MasterCard _____Visa
Account # _____
Expiration Date _____
Signature_____

| **Mail or Call:** |
| Cookbook Resources |
| 541 Doubletree Drive |
| Highland Village, TX 75077 |
| Toll Free (866) 229-2665 |
| Fax   (972) 317-6404 |

Name _____
Address_____
City_____State_____Zip_____
Telephone (Day)_____(Evening)_____

To Order: **Busy Woman's Quick & Easy Recipes**

Please send_____ hardcover copies @ $19.95 (U.S.) each $ _____
Texas residents add sales tax @ $1.65 each $ _____
Plus postage/handling @ $6.00 (1st copy) $ _____
$1.00 (each additional copy) $ _____

Check or Credit Card (*Canada-credit card only*)   Total $ _____

Charge to:
_____ MasterCard _____Visa
Account # _____
Expiration Date _____
Signature_____

| **Mail or Call:** |
| Cookbook Resources |
| 541 Doubletree Drive |
| Highland Village, TX 75077 |
| Toll Free (866) 229-2665 |
| Fax   (972) 317-6404 |

Name _____
Address_____
City_____State_____Zip_____
Telephone (Day)_____(Evening)_____

Order online at www.cookbookresources.com